# PRAISE FOR *STANDING UP*

D1413458

A beautiful journey, this story is an inspiring example of how to walk through the trials of life with your head up and shoulders back and how to learn to seek the Lord on your path. I was encouraged to be stronger and more resilient and free spirited as I read through challenges, changes, and adventures. This book is a great example of how to live with a tender mother's heart, but also as a strong individual woman, sharing and loving life with those around us. I enjoyed feeling like a missionary as I experienced Holly's journey!

*—Sharalee, CPA*

Through unimaginable tribulations, heart-wrenching trials, and deep despair, Holly discovers Jesus Christ and His incredible mercy, peace, and hope. In her story, God reveals His plans and takes her on a journey of emotional, physical, mental, and spiritual growth as she surrenders her will to His. This book will leave you in tears yet rejoicing humbly at the foot of the cross where you will be blessed beyond measure.

*—Leah Lee, educator and author of*
*young adult fiction*

*Standing Up* shows not only the fierce love of a mama's heart but the love and surrender of a woman who learned to trust God, never backing down from the devastation of sickness that wreaked havoc in her son's life. Holly draws from a fountain of strength of trust in God that surprises even her. Holly tells about the deep losses in her life and how God showed up inexplicably to always show Himself faithful and true. She follows the call on her life and reaches beyond her own pain to embrace the lost and forgotten in this world.

—*Therese Trantow, MOPS mentor*

Such an astonishing, fully surrendered walk of faith! Life is not perfect. Holly shows us how to walk through it with God. This book is an encouragement, inspiration, and points directly to our Savior, Jesus.

—*Melody Finney*

Alas! I am a woman of wobbly faith. Sometimes I feel deep connection with God, and sometimes I feel alone in the universe. Holly Conwell's *Standing Up* came "by chance" into my life to pick my faith up, dust if off, and put it front and center in my ordinary, everyday existence. Holly's faith gently reminds me that God's lessons and love are available always and everywhere – in the daffodils I bought at the market this morning, in the chance words of a stranger, in the tear drops of a friend whose mother is dying – and that to receive them, I have only to look and to listen.

—*DC Donahue,* teacher, writer, editor

# STANDING UP

A Testimony of
God's Pursuing Love

# STANDING UP

## Holly Conwell

ILLUMIFY
MEDIA.COM

# STANDING UP

Published by
Illumify Media Global
www.IllumifyMedia.com
*"We bring your book to life!"*

Library of Congress Control Number: 2021906461

Paperback ISBN: 978-1-947360-94-5
eBook ISBN: 978-1-947360-95-2

Typeset by Art Innovations (http://artinnovations.in/)
Cover design by Debbie Lewis

*Printed in the United States of America*

# CONTENTS

*Foreword*                                              vii

*Author's Note*                                         xi

1.  About to Explode                                    1

2.  Cry in the Wilderness                               15

3.  The Great Escape                                    16

4.  What is Going On?                                   21

5.  A Sixth Sense                                       26

6.  Jedd                                                29

7.  Identity Crisis                                     54

8.  Laurae                                              58

9.  No More Honey in the Honey Pot                      66

10. On a Mission to Find a Mission                      68

11. Crossroads                                          74

12. Israel                                              81

13. India                                              84

14. No Thank You—I'd Rather Not                         90

15. My Home That Is No Longer My Home                   94

16. Land of the Unexpected                              127

17. In Over My Head                                     143

18. Ruined for the Ordinary                             152

19. Respite                                             158

20. Adventures in Paradise                              160

21. Meanwhile, Back in the USA                          180

22. Growing Weary                           184
23. Bittersweet                             187
24. "You Should Write A Book"               192
25. Standing Up                             194
26. Are You Searching?                      198

**Afterword:** *My Birth Place, of All Places*   201
*About the Author*                          206

# FOREWORD

On our distracted planet of huge television screens and a hundred billion dollar entertainment industry, where cellphones illuminate nearly 6 billion human faces, connecting us with the world but severing our connection with the people around us, where we can get anything we want if we want it with a credit card and a cursor click, often with free two-day shipping, where flash, glamor, greed, and the perceived security of material things shackle us in a frantic, unlovely cycle of getting and spending, Holly Conwell's voice speaks to us quietly as from a distance, inviting us into her story where God communicates through visions, stirrings, song lyrics, flyers, and the sublimity of the natural world. Holly invites us to slow way down, to closely observe what and who is literally right in front of us, to look deeply enough, patiently enough, and faithfully enough to discern the presence, the will and the still small voice of God, ever present in all of it.

Welcome to *Standing Up*, the story of a woman stunned by life and bereft of hope who staggers onto a rocky Colorado trail with deep soul-longing in her heart, who surrenders, raises her face to God and is graced with a response.

*Standing Up* encompasses the full human condition: birth and death, love and dissolution, faith and doubt, the balance between action and rest, the adventure of travel and the wisdom of staying put. It takes us from the American Midwest to Hawaii, Israel, India, Australia, Africa to mud-slick trails through tropical jungles in Papua New Guinea, and finally drops us back in Colorado in the utterly ordinary present moment (which, you will find, shimmers steadily as a potential beginning for some new adventure of the soul).

To many people, the events in Holly Conwell's life would be sure cause for despair and the disruption of faith—many have been bowled over and plowed under by events less grave than what happens here, but not Holly.

Holly's story, like memory itself, casts a wide net, chooses a starting point that feels momentous, meanders forward, loops back on itself, highlights this or that moment or episode, then ties all the loose threads together into a tidy tale of inspiration and redemption. In the end, it leaves us with a richly textured tapestry of events, a detailed picture of a portion of a simple human life which is prayerfully, thoughtfully, and often humorously lived and relived in the telling.

In this story, as in life itself, there are several strands of things happening, none of them separate and distinct from the others, all inextricably intertwined. It is true that whenever we remember and tell a story we have to start *somewhere,* and we have to end *somewhere* and what happens in between can do loop de loops. So it is with *Standing Up,* where you will find that Chapters 6 through 10 all recount the same period of time but focus on different aspects of its transformational events. Don't worry too much over dates and times in that section . . . just let it wash over you and trust that all the pieces will fall together into a cohesive impression of a life lived in God.

Throughout the book, Holly fans the flame of the reader's faith (whether that is a smoldering, dying ember or a lively fire) with stories of how God has made His presence known and operative in her life. We get to live vicariously as Holly travels to far parts of the globe where she connects with people sorely in need of God's love and where she offers herself time and time again to be His feet, hands, and mouthpiece in the world. We are fortunate to witness her doing all this with the humble gentleness of a grandmother, faith like a mountain, the intermittent doubt of the merely human, and with boundless love for her fellow travelers on the human path.

This book is good news for three kinds of people: it is for anyone who suffers or struggles or sustains the blows of life, whether they have no faith at all or have lost it, whether they have doubts and only a dim sense of an unmarked path forward, or whether they are the fortunate possessors of a great and towering faith. All three types will find sustenance and renewed hope in the telling and testimony of what happens here.

Throughout *Standing Up*, you will find that Holly is a careful observer of the natural world, finding significance in the smallest things, welcoming with an open heart and mind the message of whatever calls her attention, considering it an invitation from God to learn something about His world and how she may be useful in it. Whether it is a butterfly, a storm, a rock, a chipmunk, the scent of plumeria, a tropical sunset or a warm saltwater wave, Holly remains receptive to the message of the will of God. In these stories, you will hear and come to recognize God's voice as Holly remembers it, and you will get practice to see how even the seemingly most insignificant events can blossom into great significance, with the simple application of faith.

In Holly's world (as in the world at large), things don't happen by accident. Throughout the book, she lands where God would have her, questions Him regularly on His sense of timing and direction for her life, catches herself at times thinking that perhaps, *just this once,* she knows better than God what is right and good for her life, always to place her life sheepishly, gracefully, and gratefully back into His capable hands. Although she sometimes drums her fingers, taps her foot, and looks at her watch, wondering when on earth God is going to finally show up, Holly always finds her way back into the understanding that He is here always, always tending, loving and dreaming for her, and for us, a good life, as a grandmother cherishes and dreams over a newborn baby.

Particularly in this early twenty-first-century world of difficulty and uncertainty, Standing Up reminds us that sometimes, what seems to be 'the end of the world' later turns out to be the beginning of something amazing, something more wonderful than we could ever have hoped for, predicted or imagined. It carries the persistent powerful reminder that what seems in one moment like unendurable hardship is later revealed as grace. Holly reminds us again and again that the reward for the search for God's presence in the world is *the peace that surpasses all understanding.*

The simple red book you have in your hands now is your personal invitation to attend to the still small voice within, to cultivate a strong connection with a faith community and the Lord of Lords, to trust God-given vision, hunch, and happenstance as reliable guides, and to be always on the lookout for what God would have you do next.

*—DC Donahue*

# AUTHOR'S NOTE

Please note: Because there were so many things happening in my life during the same time frame, I have chosen to write about each major situation as a separate 'story' so as not to be too confusing. I hope. Please keep in mind as you read chapters 6 through 10, the events in them are really intertwined within each other.

# 1

## |ABOUT TO EXPLODE|

Life was not turning out the way I had envisioned on the day, twenty years earlier, when I had said "I do." Tell me, whatever happened to white picket fences, perfect children and happily ever after?

I suspected something was not quite right for several months. Joyful and full of laughs one minute and ready to snap your head off the next. We tiptoed around as if walking on eggshells. Dark circles under his eyes, but he slept more than he was awake. Teenage boys are always hungry but not Jedd. He turned down many a meal and avoided sitting at the dinner table with us. His grades revealed he was not doing what he was capable of. Our son had become a recluse behind his bedroom door.

The moon was high in the sky; I was exhausted. Weary-eyed, I glanced at the clock and wondered who would be calling at this hour. *Now what?*

That cold February night in 2007, at the high school Valentine's dance, Jedd, in emotional despair over the betrayal of a long-time friend began to react in what the principal described over the phone as a seizure.

In the days following the "episode," my precious boy became physically, mentally, and emotionally debilitated. One morning before school I found him glaze-eyed and unfocused, barely able to utter a whisper let alone move. On a frantic call to the small, local clinic, we were advised to take him directly to the ER at the nearest hospital, a seventy-mile drive from our home. It was all my husband could do to hoist his listless son out of bed, up the stairs, and into the car.

"What is the name of the patient we will be seeing this morning?" asked the young lady behind the check-in desk.

Several people were already seated in the ER waiting room.

"And what seems to be wrong with Jedd?" she inquired while making notations on a clipboard.

"Well, just look at him!" I exclaimed in quite a rude voice, which was uncharacteristic of me—but there was nothing about this scene that was normal. Surely, they could recognize just by looking at Jedd that he was severely depressed.

I felt like an unopened soda can that had just been violently shaken. One little crack in the tab and I would spew over a number of unsuspecting innocent bystanders.

*What is taking so long?* I wondered. Scared and nervous, I sat, a whirlwind of thoughts spinning through my mind, none that I can remember now. Jedd had been taken into a room, alone, for questioning. *Why?*

A stocky, clean-cut gentleman in uniform and packing a gun at his hip escorted my husband and me into a small room, bare except for a low, padded bed and one chair. We were asked to wait there. My husband took the chair. Feeling weak and unable to stand, I sunk to the floor, pulling my knees snuggly to my chest. *Good Grief!* Shortly, Jedd staggered in with the help of an important looking hospital official. He made himself as comfortable as possible on the cold vinyl bed. The armed officer had stationed himself directly outside the meagerly furnished room, his eyes on us at all times. I felt like a criminal waiting for sentencing.

"Mr. and Mrs. Conwell," the important looking person began, "your son is suicidal. He has a plan and refuses to disclose it at this time. This implies he still may be considering following through. He is a very high-risk case, and by law, since he is a minor, we have to admit him to a mental health facility for evaluation and counseling."

My heart stopped mid-beat before dropping into the pit of my stomach. The tiny bit of breakfast I had in my belly was on the verge of regurgitation. In a split second my life had flipped upside down, inside out, and sideways.

Stunned silence. And then the tornado in my mind raged on: *Why hadn't I done something earlier? I should've seen the signs as serious red flags. How could it be that our once happy-go-lucky little boy would be contemplating taking his own life? What kind of parent am I anyway?*

Hours later, we left our son whom we love and raised in the hands and care of a juvenile mental rehabilitation center. Other boys, some older and some younger, looked curiously at the new kid wondering what his story was and how he came to be in this place. Stripped of his belt, shoelaces, and any other potentially harmful belongings,

Jedd was led to his room. We were given a list of specific instructions, things to do at home to ensure Jedd's well-being in the days to come.

That evening and over the next few days we scoured every room in the house looking for sharp objects, ropes, and knives of all sorts and sizes. In silence, we filled several cardboard boxes with anything that might become a tool of self-destruction. You can imagine what a chore this might have been, considering that my husband was an avid hunter and martial arts enthusiast. We taped the boxes shut, loaded them into the truck and removed them from the property. *Oh boy!*

## THE EARLY YEARS

While pregnant with Jedd, I managed a flower shop in a King Soopers grocery store in Fort Collins, Colorado. The sweet aroma of fresh roses, carnations, freesia, and other fragrant flowers welcomed me to work each day. Designing floral arrangements for the display coolers and special occasions gave me a creative outlet. It was gratifying work, and it kept me busy. I could hardly wait for new shipments of houseplants to arrive every couple of weeks. Before I put them out for sale, I carefully selected a few unusual species or particularly nice ones to adopt for myself. Adding to my collection was a necessary evil I could not resist.

I had every intention of returning to work after my maternity leave, but after holding the handsome little guy I couldn't bear the thought of leaving this precious new baby boy with a sitter. Thankfully, my husband's salary as a maintenance technician at the new Anheuser Busch Brewery allowed me to stay home.

Laurae was born twenty months later, and we bought a house in Bellvue, Colorado, on a sunny hill near Lory State Park and Horsetooth Reservoir. There we enjoyed hikes on the many trails and, once in a while, we made an outing to the lake for tubing behind our boat. The huge, fenced backyard made an ideal place for the kids to run and play. We tilled a garden plot in which I could play. The house came with a shop—or the shop came with a house, depending on who you ask. Either way, my husband also had his place to play.

After seven years of grueling shift work and extended mandatory work hours at Budweiser, as well as an increasingly stressful home atmosphere, we decided a move would resolve everything. (The brewery's four to six cases of free beer each month hadn't proved very helpful and only added to the challenge.) After we'd traveled around some without finding the perfect place, my father offered us a family plot high in the Sangre de Cristo Mountains in southern Colorado, twelve miles from Westcliffe. We began to build our dream home, which turned into a five-year project from the ground up.

We did everything ourselves. The only tasks we hired out were the installation of the septic system and the excavation for the foundation. We acquired permits to cut dead standing beetle-kill trees in the forest to use as posts and beams. My job included peeling the bark off the logs with a draw knife. We used alternative building methods, including straw-bale construction. I mixed the stucco and slathered it onto the bales of straw, which were stacked two stories high. (Being afraid of heights I only got the bottom layers.) I wasn't good for much else as far as construction goes. I hammered a few nails, (and my finger, splitting it open), painted a few walls, and completed a few other simple projects. My husband had majored in art at college, and this house was his biggest sculpture, a work of art for sure.

We moved in when Jedd and Laurae were in the third and second grades. I often volunteered in their classrooms and when a paid position opened up for an aide, I jumped at the opportunity. That job eventually led to my employment in the Learning Lab in the Custer County Consolidated School.

Even as a child, Jedd cared deeply for his friends and was sensitive to the feelings of others. It was not unusual to see him shed a few tears if he noticed someone else being hurt or crying. The words and actions of others affected him deeply. For the most part, though, as a young lad, Jedd was happy, full of life and energy, ornery at times, and he displayed a goofy sense of humor.

Unfortunately, he revealed a mean streak when it came to his little sister. He could be downright cruel to her. It broke my heart. I couldn't understand the aggression toward her and didn't quite know how to handle it. At one point I told Jedd that he was going to wish he had been nicer to her because someday he may need her. Little did he know how true those words would be.

The boy loved to eat. He would try just about anything put in front of him. For that I gave thanks because I read cookbooks like novels and enjoyed trying new recipes on a regular basis. He and my husband were willing guinea pigs. Laurae, not so much. An extremely picky eater at an early age, she chose never to eat meat again after seeing a skinned deer hanging from the rafters in the shop. Eyes bulging and a ridiculously long pink tongue dangling from the side of its mouth ruined her appetite.

As the kids grew, I missed the days of reading the same books over and over again. Dr. Suess, the Berenstain Bears, and Mercer Mayer.

I missed watching Jedd and Laurae jump on the trampoline, tumble on the gymnastics mats in organized chaos, launch themselves into the foam pit, and improve their swimming skills. I missed the jujitsu classes we took together as a family. I missed the silly and creative stories Jedd came up with. He loved science, experimenting, taking things apart and putting them back together. No longer did we enjoy full days of hiking, fishing, and exploring and the dinner picnics on the floor, watching a movie when my husband worked late. I missed the little boy in the backyard shooting his sling shot and bow and arrows at targets, just like his daddy.

"UH OH, Mama! I had an accident," he wailed one day as he took my hand and led me to the gravel driveway where my red 1990 Toyota Corolla was parked. He stopped at the back of the car, head down and eyes on the ground. Crumbling piece by piece, little piles of glittering glass were still falling in the two car seats that were securely fastened in the back seat.

"I shot a rock up in the air. I didn't know it was going to come down on your car," Jedd explained between sobs.

I should've been more patient and understanding of the accident that just occurred. But no. In those days I often found myself screaming at the top of my lungs, saying things that never should have escaped my mouth, only to cry myself to sleep at night in regret at the lack of self-control and the ugly words I spoke over my children. I would apologize, but I could not take back what was already said.

Why wasn't I more forgiving? Things like that happen with kids, right?

A blink of an eye and it was all gone, a memory.

# FAST-FORWARD

After our trip to the juvenile mental health center, the stress level at home escalated to an all-time high. My marriage was in dire straits. I ignored the real and perceived problems for way too long and pretended that if I didn't think about them, they would disappear or magically get better on their own. I avoided confrontation like the plague. Obviously, that wasn't working out very well.

I knew very little about depression, but boy oh boy, I was in for quite a learning experience—a course that would drag out for months. Jedd attended weekly counseling sessions and had multiple visits with the psychiatrist who would evaluate and prescribe anti-depressants, sleeping aids, and anti-psychotic meds, all with possible horrible side effects. Initially, finding the right medicine and the right dose proved to be a nightmare. I cringed as my six-foot tall, one hundred fifty-pound son stomped up the wood plank staircase with a five iron in his hands and hatred in his eyes and snapped the golf club in half like a toothpick right in front of me. I knew something was terribly wrong! This was not my Jedd! Shaking with fear, not knowing his next move, I encouraged him as calmly as I could in the moment to go outside and beat up one of the many trees on our property. As soon as the door closed behind him, I phoned the crisis hotline. *HELP!* My soda can could not explode right now. I needed to somehow hold it together.

A whirlwind constantly raged within the confines of my head. *Would Jedd wake up in the morning? Will he be home for dinner? Will I get to watch him grow into an adult, get married, and have children of his own? Will he ever be normal again? What about my marriage?*

Poor Laurae, I inadvertently neglected her in all of the chaos. Day after day after day.

My position in the Learning Lab at the school was my safe place, and I somehow managed to maintain my composure and do my job well. Whether that was actually the case, I don't know. No one ever told me otherwise. I loved working with small groups of elementary students, helping them progress to the next reading level. I found it rewarding and satisfying. The school counselor, principal, and one co-worker were the only ones I confided in about my current turmoil at home.

By now the stigma of mental illness hit Jedd hard. Rejected by friends (and their parents), he was treated as though he carried some highly contagious disease. He dreaded going to school; the abuse was real. Fear of suicide still tormented me. We were not out of the woods yet.

The rank smell of dirty socks, sweaty T-shirts laced with Axe Deodorant, days-old food, and other odors permeated Jedd's room. *Ugh!* It must be done. A broom in one hand and antibacterial spray in the other, I waded in. *How can anyone live like this?* Presumably, spilled Mountain Dew glued his jeans to the floor. A full load of dirty laundry was piled up in the corner. Apparently, he had been drawing on his pants with a red marker again. How many times had I asked him not to write on his clothes?

*Wait. That's not marker!*

I was about ready to throw out the little black film can with the rest of the garbage when suddenly I stopped. I could hear something rattling inside. My heart sank as I counted one, two, three . . . ten white pills. Why was he not taking the antidepressants? Could he be saving them? What was he thinking? *Good grief.*

Undeniably familiar, the foul smell wafted through the bathroom door. Nasty Marlboros. I started smoking at age sixteen too. Thought it was cool and people accepted you if you were cool. But that kind of cool led me to experimenting with weed, alcohol, and other drugs and behaviors that definitely were not cool.

For the first time in what seemed forever, Jedd and I carried on a deep and meaningful conversation. Yes, he had started smoking. He enjoyed it, and it calmed his anxiety. He didn't like taking the pills. The medicine made him feel like a zombie walking aimlessly through the course of each day with relatively no emotion, good or bad. The cutting was short-lived, thankfully. It saddened me to learn that the pain from self-inflicted wounds took his mind off the emotional pain he suffered. He would rather endure the physical pain. We discussed the reasons and sources of the hurt and feelings that triggered the depression. In group counseling they were addressing these issues, and Jedd felt relieved in a sense that he was not alone. I held on to hope I would get my son back someday.

During those difficult times, I daydreamed of days not so long ago. It was school picture day, and the middle-schoolers were lining up outside the auditorium waiting their turn. My small reading group and I were in the all-purpose room adjacent to the auditorium. In the middle of a lesson Jedd jumped into the room, startling myself and the kiddos.

"How do I look?" he asked excitedly in a not-so-inside voice.

*Absolutely ridiculous*, I thought. Normally his dark wavy hair was kept neatly brushed and hung slightly above the collar. His eyes matched his hair color while his smile looked like many others his age: silver brackets on each white tooth decorated with the newest colors of miniature rubber bands. The brighter the better. The children wanted to know who the big boy was who put so many ponytails all over his head. I chuckled to myself at his silliness. (I quit ordering school pictures the following year and vowed never to order any more when the goofball decided to gargle with red food coloring right before the big "cheese.")

Another time I recalled the moment I heard Jedd's voice echo through Walmart. His new manly voice was randomly interrupted by a high pitch squeal.

"Mommy! Mommy, where are you? I can't see you Mommy!"

Running out from the cereal aisle, a tall lanky boy with a smirk appeared. "Oh, Mommy! I've been looking all over for you!"

A big hug and both my feet came off the ground. While being twirled around I scanned the area. Did I know anyone who just witnessed Jedd make a spectacle of himself, and of me?

I can't forget taking Jedd and a group of his friends to Pueblo for the day, just to hang out. Crossing the intersection in front of Denny's, I heard a roar of laughter behind me that sounded suspicious. After quickly glancing over my shoulder I pretended to have no idea who these "not quite adult" kids belonged to. Jedd's fluorescent green Tripps pants, with the extra-large pockets and decorative chains, were wrapped around his ankles, dragging in the street. Thank goodness for the oversized T-shirt as he waddled to the curb where he dramatically began to re-dress himself.

Oh, the memories. Yep, that was my darling son. The one who could embarrass me and make me laugh at the same time. I hoped and longed for a return to goofy.

Thursday afternoons in the Learning Lab were my designated planning periods at school. I loved my job, the children, and my coworkers. A fun bunch, and I learned heaps about early childhood development and education. One particular Thursday, September 20, 2007, I sat at my desk making lesson plans. Sets of children's guided reading books stacked in piles by grade level covered the desktop. I carefully planned a reading, writing, and comprehension piece to each lesson. I was deep in concentration when an unexpected knock at the door caused me to jump. My handsome son confidently walked over and handed me piece of paper. I couldn't believe what I was reading. Was this legal? Can he really do this? *Good grief! I give up!* I wasn't going to argue or get angry. *I'm tired of fighting.*

"Jedd, fine," I said with a sigh. "But I will not allow you to sit at home and do nothing. You have to find a job."

Apparently in Colorado, a student can quit school at age seventeen without a parent's consent. He didn't waste any time. It was his birthday.

Within a week he found a job washing dishes and prepping food at a local restaurant.

## LOST IN THE CHAOS

While all my energy and focus was on what was happening with Jedd, I failed to meet the needs of Laurae in this crucial time of her young life. Unbeknownst to me, she began to resort to her own methods of self-preservation. It started with smoking marijuana with her friends behind the laundromat near the school. *How did I not know that?* At fourteen, she was trying to find her identity in the world in the midst of girlish drama and peer pressure. I could relate as I had not handled the all-consuming struggles of adolescence very well. Everything had seemed to be a life-or-death crisis in my own immature mind. Eventually sex, drugs, and rock-n-roll became my crutch and my false sense of self-worth and happiness. How was I going to raise a healthy, confident, and morally sound young lady when I myself had been a failure?

Homecoming week was always a big event in little ole Westcliffe. Activities and dress up days at the school during the week and ending with a parade and the football game on Friday. Homecoming royalty, all decked out in their formal gowns and suits, waved proudly from the chauffeured convertible at the people lining the streets. Horses strutted down Main Street followed by the marching band, police cars, firetruck, and class floats all vying for the best in show. A flatbed truck pulling the freshman float slowed down at the end of the road, and a few of the students, Laurae's classmates, jumped off to walk alongside. A small crowd of fifty or so spectators, adults and children, were still lingering in the streets when the unthinkable happened.

Laurae had hung out with friends in town that day. My husband was presumably tinkering in his shop while Jedd enjoyed playing video games with a few friends. I liked how he and his buddies felt comfortable hanging out at the house. At least I knew where he was. I chose to stay home that day—probably catching up on laundry, house cleaning, and watering my large collection of house plants.

The jingle of the landline interrupted the task at hand and drew me to the kitchen.

"What? Slow down, take a deep breath, and tell me again," I said while trying to make sense of the frantic words on the other end of the line.

"The truck . . . ran . . . over her. She was trying to . . . get back . . . on the float. Mom, she fell . . . and the truck ran over her," Laurae exclaimed.

"Oh my gosh, Laurae. Are you OK? Where are you?" I questioned.

"Yes, I'm OK." The jitters in her voice told me she was pretty shaken up. "Everyone is in the school gym. They say she will be alright."

News came later that the girl did not survive the crushing weight of the truck.

First the trauma of her older brother being on the verge of suicide and now the traumatic death of a classmate.

*What else could possibly go wrong?*

# 2

## CRY IN THE WILDERNESS

Come fall of 2007, desperation forced me out the front door of our beautiful log home in the Sangre de Cristo Mountains. My feet stumbled as I staggered along the familiar hiking trails through the pine tree forest. My mind disappeared in a thick fog, tears streamed down my cheeks, and my heart lay broken in pieces. *When would this bad dream end?* Feeling hopeless and losing control, I stopped and gazed at my surroundings with blurred vision, barely able to stand up, seriously wishing I could just run away from this nightmare. All the pent-up fizz inside me had just about fizzled out. Instead, I subconsciously tilted my head back, scanned the blue sky overhead, and cried out from deep within my soul. "God, if you are real, You are going to have to show me a sign. I cannot do this anymore!"

In anticipation I looked around half expecting one of the little shrubs along the path to burst into flames. But . . . nothing. Absolutely nothing.

Yet!

# 3

## THE GREAT ESCAPE

It took Jedd only about three months to come to the conclusion that he should probably go back to school, but he refused to return to school in Westcliffe. Everyone knew his story, and the stigma of mental illness is brutal. In a way, I didn't blame him. Within a sixty-mile radius of Westcliffe there were three school options. Being mid-winter with snowy and icy roads, I didn't like the idea of him driving one hundred twenty miles a day alone. He still wasn't emotionally stable and that continually worried me. Suddenly, a brilliant idea came to mind. *I could move with him. Yes! A new beginning for him and a great escape for me from the turmoil overtaking my life. And after he graduated, I could go back to Westcliffe and attempt to save my marriage.* Sounded like a fantastic plan. I was excited, relieved, and nervous all at the same time. Laurae decided she wanted to go too.

I applied for a leave of absence at my work as a reading intervention assistant, and my request was granted. *What was I thinking?* Moving with the kids on a rash decision with no job and no guarantee of what was to come. I felt unstable and desperate. I wasn't thinking, actually. I didn't consider the impact and hurt it was going to cause my husband, the kids' father.

On January 2, 2008, we packed up a few necessary belongings and moved into a small two-bedroom duplex in Cañon City. Jedd and Laurae each occupied the bedrooms upstairs while I stayed in the living room. My twin bed served as a couch as well. The duplex proved comfortable enough and within walking distance to the high school and downtown area. We also brought our fluffy, spastic but loving and loyal Pomeranian, Diego. We didn't have a fenced yard, which meant one of us would have to walk him several times a day. That soon became a burden I couldn't deal with.

## BACK IN SCHOOL, ALL OF US

Jedd liked being anonymous at the big school in Cañon City, which accommodated approximately two thousand students compared to two hundred in his previous school. He reconnected with some friends he had known earlier. He still struggled with depression but was optimistic, and so was I. Laurae on the other hand adjusted slowly to the larger school and had trouble making new friends.

After only a couple months, Jedd started having anxiety attacks at school. He didn't like the way his medication made him feel and chose not to take it. That's so frustrating! *Rugabugs.* He quit school again and applied to an alternative school in the same town. It turned out to be a great decision. He was accepted and thrived. In fact, he liked it so much, Laurae wanted to give it a try. She liked the idea of working at her own pace (she was a lot more disciplined than Jedd) and believed if she really focused and worked hard maybe she could graduate early.

It took me a couple months of job searching before I was hired at a charter school as a third-grade teaching assistant. It was a good fit, and I enjoyed the children, the staff, and the atmosphere at the school. It seemed very positive, and I longed for that.

The first week of school, maybe even the first day, while I was on recess duty, a sweet little girl with a blond ponytail cheerfully asked me what church I went to. "Well, sweetie, I don't go to church," I responded.

"Then you should come to the Vineyard. There's coffee and donuts," she replied with confidence. I smiled, maybe even chuckled, and said, "OK" with no intention whatsoever of going.

## THE VINEYARD

Over the next six or seven months, the strangest things kept happening. I had never heard of a Vineyard church before, but for some reason I began hearing about it constantly, seeing flyers and advertisements here and there and even receiving invitations on my door to come check it out. The church was only two blocks from where we lived. Laurae and I laughed about how it just kept *popping up*. One day I came home to a small Ziploc bag of homemade cookies on my front step with a note from the Vineyard. Little did I know at the time, God was giving me a sign, the sign I cried out for in desperation months earlier.

Over the summer break Laurae and I worked on an organic farm for a weekly share of food. It was absolutely relaxing and therapeutic, something I needed and enjoyed. I always loved gardening with the warm sunshine on my back and the fresh produce. Warm cucumbers right off the vine are the best.

Jedd found a job at a local coffee shop as a dishwasher and prep cook. He was glad to have something to do, and a paycheck. He socialized more often, and his ambition slowly returned. My heart felt delighted for him.

My heart also felt something else—a nagging conviction. I had told that precious little girl I would go to church. I don't like to tell people I will do something and not follow through. It really bothered me even though she had long forgotten our short little conversation on the playground. It was weird, though, I couldn't ignore the feeling. Finally, no question about it, I had to go.

After my first service at the Vineyard, I was pleasantly surprised. There was no judgment or papers to sign. The music was live , and the atmosphere was informal and no pressure. I watched curiously as people sang with their hands raised, swaying and dancing or standing quietly with their eyes closed as if in another world. I never experienced anything quite like it. It was different and intriguing. I wanted to go again, and so I did . . . again and again. One Sunday after the sermon, the pastor made an announcement. He invited those people who wanted to accept Jesus as their Lord and Savior to come forward. I wasn't really sure what that meant, but a strange desire welled up in me, and I was curious to find out. The thought of walking up and standing in front of the congregation made me uncomfortable, so I stayed put and watched.

That night while lying in bed, I admitted that I made lots of mistakes and poor ungodly choices, and I asked God to forgive me. I wanted to give Jesus a try because I had heard that "if you confess with your mouth that Jesus is Lord and believe in your heart that God raised him from the dead, you will be saved. For with the heart one believes and is justified, and with the mouth one confesses and is saved" (Romans 10:9-10). And that was that. No fireworks, bells, or whistles. Just a simple prayer of repentance and a few tears of relief. I was forty-seven years old.

# 4

## WHAT IS GOING ON?

As the days and weeks went by, I noticed changes in my attitude and behavior. The desire to drink alcohol of any kind disappeared. I was bothered and upset by the foul language that spilled from my mouth and the mouths of others. I found myself more relaxed and not stressing about things that were out of my control. I felt sturdier, more sure-footed, and embraced a peace I could not explain. My life circumstances remained the same, but how I responded to them changed. God was transforming me from the inside out.

People will tell you that your life will never be the same after you are saved. It is true and for the better. Very few will tell you, though, that there will be trials and tribulations (John 16:33). The Bible doesn't say that there *might* be trials but that there *will* be. *Good grief.* Hadn't I already experienced enough of life's difficulties?

# BUZZZZ

As long as the weather was nice that fall, Laurae and I continued working weekends at the farm. I remember one particular day we spent on our knees digging and harvesting potatoes. Even though it was close to one hundred degrees, we covered our arms, legs, and heads with lightweight clothing as a barrier against mosquitos. Still the ferocious little buggers found their way under our collars, hats, and inside our sleeves. They were determined to bite and fill their tiny bellies with our blood. They were relentless and succeeded despite our efforts to deter them. We itched for days afterward.

About two weeks later, Laurae became very ill. She had a critically high fever, severe headaches, and aches and pains that would not go away. It was unlike her to get that sick and not recover within a few days. She needed to see a doctor. Believing it to be a standard virus, the doctor prepared to send us home to ride it out when I remembered those vicious mosquitos. "Could it possibly be West Nile Virus?" I asked the doctor.

Several days later, tests confirmed it was in fact West Nile. Unfortunately, there is not a cure, only medicine for treating the symptoms. We scheduled a CT scan to make sure no excessive swelling in the brain occurred. I did some research and discovered that people and horses can die from West Nile. A mother's worst nightmare is that she might outlive her children. No! I refused to allow that to happen. Not with Jedd and not now with Laurae. I prayed.

# MR. B

Not long after the West Nile scare, I took Diego out for his nightly bedtime walk. The lampposts dimly lit up the dark streets and not many people were out, so I wasn't too concerned about being seen in my pink polka-dot flannel pajama pants. I wasn't planning a long walk, just a route I had taken several times before. I knew the houses where the friendly dogs lived and avoided the ones that were questionable. A Basenji lived in the neighborhood behind a chain-link fence, and in the past he never seemed bothered by us walking by. That night, though, he appeared obviously agitated. Basenjis don't bark, but he ran back and forth in a frenzy along the inside of the fence. To be cautious, I led Diego into the middle of the street as we strolled by. Diego could sense something and began to bark. Somehow, somewhere Mr. Basenji worked his way under the fence and ran directly toward us. My first thought was to pick up Diego to avoid a dog fight, but I didn't move quick enough. Instead, Mr. B's jaw clamped down on my left leg just below my calf and shook it around like a rag doll. As quickly as he'd attacked, he released his grip and ran away. It happened so fast. All I can say is he must not have liked my pink PJ's. With blood dripping down into my shoe, I limped the two blocks home. I examined my injury and decided maybe I should make a trip to the ER. Yep, and it's a good thing. I got twelve stitches plus two nice canine puncture wounds.

In hindsight I wish I had worn real pants and shaved my legs more recently. The photos for the police report were kind of embarrassing.

## "UNTIL DEATH DO YOU PART"

When we first moved to Cañon City, the kids and I made a
point to go home to Westcliffe on the weekends. It was awkward
and uncomfortable and conversation between me and my husband
couldn't have been much less. As time went on, our trips became
fewer and farther between. At one point, my husband said he was
beginning to like living alone. "O, Lord," I prayed. "What am I to do
with our marriage?" One of the clearest messages I had ever received
from God was this one: *until death do you part*. Oh my, how could
that ever work out? Honestly, I wasn't sure if I wanted to stay married.

## ME?! MISSIONS??

I continued to faithfully attend church on Sundays. Several
times I even bribed the kids with twenty dollars each to come with
me. Money talks to teenagers, and I desperately wanted them to
know Jesus too. The work God was doing inside of me proved to
be incredible, and though it didn't make sense, I felt like a totally
different and new person (2 Corinthians 5:17). My confidence level
increased, and for the first time in a long time I believed I could stand
on my own two feet. I could never have done it on my own. I had
tried all that I knew to do and had failed.

One particular Sunday, the gist of the message included this
question: What is my personal mission? In the pastor's closing prayer,
he asked for the Holy Spirit to come and place a desire upon our
hearts to become a pastor, teacher, or missionary. (*The Holy Spirit?
Hmmm*. I heard about it before but never fully understood. I was

being introduced to so much that my mind couldn't contain or comprehend it all.) I stood there thinking how exciting it would be to be a missionary, to travel around the world and help serve hungry orphans. *Sure, I could do that.* (How's that for my limited knowledge of missions?)

Then, out of nowhere, my body started to shake like an internal earthquake. I looked at my hands, but they appeared motionless. They began to sweat. *What was going on?* I could feel my heart pounding inside my chest. Just then, the pastor explained we would know if the Holy Spirit was speaking to us if we felt sensations like sweaty palms, shaking, and a rapid heartbeat. Whoa! Really! I was experiencing all three. Never in my life!

"Would those people please come forward for prayer?" I heard the pastor say.

OK, this time I did it, although somewhat reluctantly. I was thankful I wasn't the only one making their way to the front. As the pastor began to pray for us, he said even then God may give us a specific country or people group to which He may be calling us to serve, teach, or minister. All I know is, in my mind's eye I saw a bunch of dark-skinned children with curly black hair. *That's awesome*, I thought. I always dreamed of going to Africa.

# 5

## A SIXTH SENSE

"**M**om, I have a feeling something bad is going to happen," Jedd said one morning before school. *Ugh. I hate it when he says things like that. The outcome is usually not good.*

After I parked and pulled the keys out of the ignition, I heard the ring of my phone inside my purse. I had just returned home from work. The woman on the other end identified herself as so-and-so, an employee in the emergency room of such-and-such hospital in Denver. Laurae had been in a serious car accident, and they needed my permission to treat her. Taking a deep breath, I asked for details, but they weren't at liberty to give me any information over the phone. *Good grief.* Now, I'm pretty sure God granted me a favor because when I asked the woman if I could speak to my daughter, she hesitated as if that was not normal practice. Without saying anything, she walked into the room where Laurae lay on the examining table and handed her the hospital phone.

Through tears and grimaces of pain, Laurae assured me she was going to be OK. "Yes, I'm alright Mom, but my butt REALLY hurts, and they want to give me morphine and I don't want any morphine." (She never did like taking medicine of any kind.)

That morning, May 13, 2009, a week before her seventeenth birthday, she and some friends left to attend an Amtgard competition, a medieval combat role-playing game with foam swords and costumes. As they drove through Denver, a car T-boned the front passenger side where Laurae sat, the position of greatest impact. It took the Jaws of Life to get her out.

In all reality I should've been a basket case. *Why am I so calm?* I thought. *My daughter just survived a horrible accident, and I am surprisingly at peace.* Again, it could only be "the peace of God, which surpasses all understanding" (Philippians 4:7).

During the three-hour drive from Cañon to Denver I prayed, thanking God for His mercy for sparing Laurae's life a second time. I sang along with the worship music that played on the radio. After several hours waiting for test results in the ER, Laurae was checked out in the wee hours of the morning. With a pair of crutches and an prescription for pain medicine for a broken tail bone and fractured pelvis (hence the sore butt), we slowly made our way to my in-laws' home in Denver for the night.

The doctors let us know that if Laurae should ever become pregnant, a natural delivery may not be a safe option due to the pelvic fractures. I rebuked that statement right away in the name of Jesus and thought, *anyway, we won't have to worry about that for a long time.*

## DEPRESSION SPEAKING?

October 6, 2009, Jedd made a remark that put a lump in my throat and a jolt through my body. He had this really strong feeling he was going to die; he could feel it coming. The feeling was so overwhelming and real he wrote a will. My first thought was he was contemplating suicide again. Although he assured me it wouldn't be at his own hand, he wasn't sure the cause of death. Still, I couldn't help thinking depression would rear its ugly head once more. *He needs Jesus,* I thought. *He needs unconditional love.*

At that moment I remembered when I had abruptly awoken from a deep sleep about a month earlier. The event disturbed me so much I wrote it down in my journal. Jedd's voice broke the silence of the night with a bad dream: "Mom, I think I have cancer!" he yelled.

That was all; I didn't hear anything else. The words were as plain as day and so matter of fact. When I had asked him the following morning, Jedd had no recollection of talking in his sleep or having a bad dream.

# 6

## JEDD

### BE STILL AND KNOW THAT I AM GOD

Pretty much from the night when I prayed that simple prayer of repentance and received my eternal salvation, I began to keep a daily journal. I am so thankful I did because without it I would not be able to write with clarity the rest of my story and give God the glory.

Just like when the Vineyard church kept popping up everywhere in random places, the Bible verse from Psalm 46:10 kept appearing to me. "Be still, and know that I am God." *That's strange*, I thought, although God seemed to be making it quite clear this was very important. Little did I know at the time how I would soon have to lean on that truth over and over. (Still do.)

Jedd ended up dropping out of the alternative school late in the fall but continued to work at the coffee shop. He decided he would just take the GED test and be done with it.

Laurae, on the other hand, worked diligently and continued on track to finish her studies early, eventually becoming the valedictorian of her graduating class. She also glowed with joy while adjusting to the changes within her body where a precious child was being "fearfully and wonderfully made" (Psalm 139:14) in her womb.

More on that surprise later.

In the meantime, Jedd complained of a lot pain in his back and right shoulder. We suspected it was job related as he spent many hours bent over washing dishes or prepping food for the cooks. By now he stood six foot two inches tall. New shoes with more support for the long hours standing, over-the-counter pain medication, and a few days off to rest his muscles should do the trick. Unfortunately, none of this solved the problem. Instead, it became worse, the pain was occasionally accompanied by bouts of vomiting. I feared he might lose his job for the increasing number of times he called in sick, especially since within a couple hours he would appear to feel fine and take the skateboard out for a ride. My concerns were confirmed, and Jedd was let go of his position. Trying to decipher what the source of the pain could be, we reasoned that maybe a fall from a previous crash on the skateboard caused some internal injury. The doctors couldn't find any logical explanation either but agreed to take some X-rays.

During Jedd and Laurae's combined graduation party (he passed his GED with flying colors), Jedd pulled me aside. "I just don't feel right Mom," he moaned. Deep dark circles outlined his beautiful brown eyes. Pale and obviously not feeling well, he sat alone for most of the celebration. He did not look healthy at all.

Pulling up his shirt, Jedd showed me his belly button protruding from his bloated belly. He normally had an innie not an outie. Feeling his abdomen, I realized right away that something was terribly wrong. It felt like the sole of a bedroom slipper lodged right under the skin. *Why hadn't he shown me this before?*

The following day Jedd showed up for an appointment with the doctor to go over the results of the X-rays. He promised he would show the doctor his stomach.

February 18, 2010, I received a call at school from Jedd. It was not like him to bother me at work. Sitting in the radiology waiting room at the hospital he reported the X-rays were normal, but the doctor had requested a CT scan immediately after examining his belly. "What did he think it was?" I inquired. Apparently, the doctor was just as stumped.

## 10 ON THE RICHTER SCALE

It was hardly thirty minutes later when I got another phone call. "Mom, I don't know what it is, but the technician said he has never seen anything like it. By the look on his face, I think he's feeling sorry for me. He said the doctor would call when he gets the results."

Once again, the ringtone interrupted my work. OK, first of all, it is unheard of to get test results back within an hour. Secondly, what could be so pressing that we needed to see the doctor right NOW? My mind racing like a gerbil in a wheel. I packed up early to meet Jedd at the physician's office. Thoughts and questions were pounding like hail inside my head. "Oh Lord, what is happening?" I prayed.

"There appears to be a very large tumor in Jedd's stomach cavity," the physician assistant began. "The swelling is very likely the cause of the pain in his back and shoulder and would also explain the vomiting."

I had no words and started to feel a bit nauseated myself.

"I have ordered a set of blood tests to be taken tonight at the lab. You have an appointment with a surgeon tomorrow morning," he continued.

He kept talking but the words just disappeared like bubbles in a bubble bath.

STOP! WAIT! Everything was happening too fast. We haven't had time to process any of this. How did a painful shoulder turn into a possible cancerous tumor? Or tumors, plural.

*Oh Lord and Holy Spirit speak to us all and comfort us in ways only You know how. You are an amazing God, and You will get us through this.*

Though the earth quakes, "I shall not be shaken" (Psalm 62:6).

## LOOKS LIKE AN OCTOPUS

Tears came silently but liberally. *What? How? Why?* Our brains could not ignore the nagging questions that tormented our sleep. In a daze, we (the whole family, my husband included) traveled from one appointment to another trying to absorb all the information and medical lingo that bombarded us from every side. Test after test after test. Seven days of continual meetings with doctors, surgeons, and oncologists. Results confirmed Jedd had a very rare form of cancer called desmoplastic small round blue cell tumor. The growth likened itself to an octopus with tentacles entangled around the intestines and other organs in Jedd's abdomen. When the surgeon showed me the black-and-white images on his computer, my untrained eye only saw unidentifiable shapes in different shades of grey.

"It's a tough one," the surgeon explained. "We are in contact with specialists in different parts of the world discussing the most effective treatment plan. A Groshong catheter will be inserted immediately into his chest to administer the chemo drugs. Jedd's treatment is scheduled to begin in a couple of days."

Despite the diagnosis, we remained positive and strong for each other. Laurae and I believed that God still performs miracles today. Jedd became a pillar of inspiration. He was handling this with a maturity that I could not comprehend. He made me proud. Unlike the time only a few short years before when I received the news of Jedd's severe depression and suicidal tendencies, when I had felt that I was ready to explode, with this new diagnosis I had an indescribable sense of hope and comfort that all would be OK. With the cancer diagnosis, I found myself standing on the only firm foundation I knew, trusting in God's faithfulness. God was my place of "refuge and strength" (Psalm 46:1). The difference in my response to the two situations is truly remarkable.

My biggest request at this time involved Jedd's salvation, whatever that might take. Lord, heal his heart first, I prayed.

## POISON

The next four months proved to be a marathon of appointments, treatments, and trying to work in between. During chemo treatments I worked half days and then drove the forty-five minutes to the hospital where I would stay until late in the evening. Many times,

Laurae came along. I was forever grateful to have her company and support. So often it would be after 10 p.m. before we'd head home. Totally exhausted, I knew the next day would be a repeat.

Each treatment involved a hospital stay of five to seven days. Upon check-in, the nurses pumped Jedd full of hydration solutions as well as the drug mesna to protect his liver and kidneys in preparation for the chemo drugs. During the five-day visits he would receive a continual drip of two chemo medicines while during the longer stays he had a combination of three different drugs. A chemo cocktail some would call it. The medicine was so potent that some of the nurses wore protective clothing and gloves while switching out the bags or flushing the catheter and tubing. The doctor told me if I were to receive the same amount and potency of the medicine they were administering to Jedd, it would kill me on the first round. *Good Grief! Sounds like poison to me.*

With not much to do while sitting in the hospital, Jedd researched this particular form of cancer on his laptop. His findings indicated that there were only nine reported cases in the U.S., and none had survived. I thought about throwing his computer out with the garbage. He thought about finding a gun or jumping off the Royal Gorge Bridge. He researched that too and, calculating the velocity of the fall, discovered it would be impossible for anyone to survive the impact.

*Oh Lord, HELP!*

"Be still and know," I recalled the words God had given me earlier.

Those who have gone through chemo know the reality of the grueling side effects: nausea, diarrhea and constipation, pain, water retention and swelling, mouth sores, nightmares and sleepless nights, severe headaches, depression, and the telltale sign of complete hair loss. What I did not expect was the perspiration beading up on his swollen legs. It felt like wax. It left a film on my hands and it didn't wash off easily. I also noticed a waxy film on the surface of the water in the toilet when he peed. What is this chemo stuff?

Four treatments down, two to go before a possible major surgery to de-bulk.

## PENNIES

The gas, food, and vanilla lattes added up as we traveled back and forth for treatments. What can I say? I love my coffee, and Jedd had a craving for it as well. My school organized a special challenge to help with these costs: "Pennies for the Conwell's." The class that brought in the most pennies would earn a pizza party. *What a beautiful gesture!* It brought tears to my eyes to see these compassionate little children bring in bags and jars full of coins, not just pennies. Parents told me stories of their sons who emptied their entire piggybanks and bank accounts to donate to the challenge. Forty-five dollars and eighty-seven dollars is a lot of money for a third-grader to part with for Jedd, a person they did not know personally. One mom admitted she tried to talk her son out of it, but he insisted on donating every cent. Another parent stopped me in the grocery store one day to tell me what his daughter had done. Little Suzy Q lost a tooth and put it under her pillow with a note to the Tooth Fairy. "Please give the money to Pennies for the Conwell's." I couldn't hold back the tears and cried right there in the produce department.

The final total at the end of the challenge amounted to just shy of fifteen hundred dollars. Incredible!

These kids not only gave financially, but they poured out their hearts on brightly decorated homemade cards and pictures that I hung on the wall by my desk. Their creative spelling cracked me up, but the sentiments were genuine. A young boy even asked if he could pray for me while we were standing in the hallway. Are you kidding me?! Turn down a prayer from a nine-year-old who wants to lay hands on me? No way!

Although we were receiving financial support for gas, food, and coffee, the biggest strain was the hospital bills. They began to escalate astronomically. No way we could afford to pay them. Each hospital admission exceeded forty-five thousand dollars and that didn't include scans, X-rays, or pain and nausea meds. In the end, God, in His grace and mercy, miraculously covered all the bills in full. He knows what we need before we ask and supplies more than we ever imagine or think (Ephesians 3:20). His love is so great.

## CALIFORNIA DREAMIN'

*In the name of Jesus, CANCER BE GONE! I think I'm losing my mind. I just want to sit in the sun and rest, worship, and pray for an entire day. I'm so tired, and I feel like I have so much to do, simple stuff like doing the dishes.*

May 5, 2010, we met with the surgeons at Children's Hospital in Denver. Again, the specialists confirmed the cancer is very rare and extremely difficult to treat. "Unfortunately, survival rate is not good," he said. "Basically, the debulking surgery is just buying us more time—six months to two years." The recommended plan of action included one more five-day continual chemo drip and then a two- to three-week break to recover and gain enough strength for surgery. After that there would be more chemo, radiation, and possibly clinical trials. We already knew Jedd's time on this earth was being cut short—despite fervent prayers for a miraculous healing—but hearing the prognosis again felt like an elephant standing on my chest.

One day into Jedd's sixth chemo treatment he suffered an excruciating headache. It wasn't the first headache he'd endured during treatments, but this was going to be his last. "I'M DONE. NO MORE CHEMO. I'M FINISHED. DONE," he told his doctor. We signed the discharge papers for the last time. Jedd agreed to have the debulking surgery but refused all future treatments. He would not let the chemo kill him. He wanted a couple good years to do what he wanted.

Jedd's last wish was to go to the ocean and that plan sparked some energy. He had taken a road trip with a foreign exchange student we'd hosted the year he suffered his mental breakdown. The boy's parents came from Germany and invited Jedd to travel with them to a number of hotspots in California. He had especially liked San Francisco and the Monterey Bay area, and he wanted to return.

You have no idea how good it made me feel when he said he wanted to make the trip with his father. Not that I didn't want to go, but it was an answer to my prayers for him to spend time with my husband, just the two of them. I have to admit that I was concerned about his physical comfort sitting in a car so long. I was also concerned he may not be able to flush out his port daily and avoid large crowds where he could get sick without warning. His immune system was still incredibly compromised. I chose to let it go and trust God to care for him. After all, He cares for us much better than we can ourselves (1 Peter 5:7).

Although the trip was cut short by a couple days because of nausea and an elevated heartbeat, I was glad he and my husband spent the time together. Plus, it gave me a chance to spend time with Laurae and give her some well-deserved undivided attention. At that time my daughter was about to have a baby. I was delighted to be a grandma and got to shop for all kinds of fun unnecessary things with which to spoil that baby! How exciting is that? Yes, it was joy in the face of adversity.

People often asked me how I was functioning with everything going on in my life. That's a good question. All I can do is give the glory to God. It's beyond me. It made no logical sense, but yet I remained standing.

*You are my rock, my strength in my weakness (2 Corinthians 12:9)*, I prayed. I cannot explain the peace in my heart nor the joy in the trials. I cried many tears, but I know God's love is greater than all things. I keep telling everyone it will be OK, and I truly believe it.

## SUMMER DAYS AND SUMMER NIGHTS

On the day of Jedd's debulking surgery, the nurses called me every hour on the hour with updates from the operating room at Children's Hospital in Denver. A very large tumor, the size of a dinner plate, was being carefully removed from the fatty tissue that lines the abdomen and organs. Next, his appendix and multiple cherry tomato-sized tumors were removed. Surgery to attempt to dislodge the hundreds of other small seeds and polyps without permanently damaging the intestines, kidneys, and bladder proved too dangerous to continue. Finally, the ten-inch vertical incision was closed up. Jedd refused any follow-up radiation or clinical trials and hoped to enjoy the rest of his life the best he could.

The days and nights tended to blend together that summer. Nearly every night I spent massaging Jedd's back and shoulders, literally an hour here and an hour there, to help relieve some of the pain. It became more and more uncomfortable for him to sleep lying down and so hospice brought in a lift chair. It was big, firm, and bulky and unfortunately quite uncomfortable. Eventually, Jedd moved into a reclining rocking chair we'd bought when he was two years old.

During the days I managed to do some cleaning and cooking for the many visitors and the occasional overnight guests that came by. My phone rang constantly, people wanting updates and offering prayer. I would guess hundreds of people were lifting us up in prayer all over the United States.

I feel like I'm in robot mode right now, I wrote in my journal. I don't want to think about anything, I just do what I am programmed to do. I guess the good Lord is programming me because I don't think I could do this on my own. I know I can't. I need His strength (Philippians 4:13). All I knew for sure at the time was I was tired. Physically, mentally, emotionally, and spiritually. Little did I know the challenges that lay ahead.

BE STILL AND KNOW THAT I AM GOD (Psalm 46:10). When I began to doubt and question and wonder how I could go on, God would lovingly and purposefully highlight that verse and put it somewhere I wouldn't miss it. Each time, it put me on my feet again.

# HEART ON PAPER

Feeling lonely and disconnected from real life, I poured my heart out. My journal detailed a plethora of prayers, questions, thoughts, angry words, desires, and emotions. Writing became an avenue of therapy and release in my world of caregiving.

*August 5, 2010*

*Oh my God, my Father, I love you. I'm clinging to You for sanity. I'm so emotional these days. It is so hard and today I feel like I'm losing it. Diego is stressing me out. I don't want to get up at 5 a.m. and take him for a walk and then again five more times throughout the day. I'm over it. I guess I'm just having a poor me pity party, and I need to get over it. It makes me grumpy. I don't feel like having company, entertaining, and coming up with meals. My husband came by to visit. He made a comment about my driving. I'm over that too. School starts in two and a half weeks, and I'm a mess.*

*August 12, 2010*

*"Always bless what God is doing," a pastor friend advised me one evening. That sure seems a strange thing to do. How do you bless what God is doing in someone's life when they are dying*

of an incurable disease? But then I remembered a verse God had highlighted and put on my heart a year or so earlier. Romans 8:28 ESV reads: "And we know that for those who love God all things work together for good, for those who are called according to his purpose." I choose to hold on to both.

## August 30, 2010

Jedd told me he had been thinking a lot about God lately and about life after death. He says he really doesn't care about his past and all the things he has; it is just stuff and it really didn't matter. "I believe in God now, Mom."

Not knowing what else to say I asked, "does that mean you know you are going to heaven?"

"Yes."

I cried. I had cried buckets of tears, but these were tears of joy! My most desperate prayers had been answered. Both of my children have called upon the name of Jesus and have been saved by grace through faith (Ephesians 2:8).

## September 10, 2010

School started August 29, but I am having a hard time focusing and concentrating on anything. Sleepless nights massaging Jedd's back and having long conversations is taking its toll on me. We really need my income, but Jedd needs me more. He asked if I could please stay home. It is the first time I sensed fear in his voice. He didn't know what was going to happen, how painful it was going to be or when. Although I had no idea of the time frame, I asked for a temporary leave of absence, and the school board agreed to save my position. I am so blessed.

## September 19, 2010

"Whatever you're doing inside of me feels like chaos, but somehow there's peace." These song lyrics by Sanctus Real played over and over in my head and accurately describe how I feel most of the time. (Throughout these trials, God spoke to me through song many a time. Words of encouragement, confirmation, hope and unfailing love.)

## October 15, 2010

"I love you, Mom. I'm so glad for the time we've been able to spend together now. I couldn't ask for a better Mom." Oh, my goodness how I needed to hear that. So many times, I considered myself a failure as a parent. I made countless mistakes and words escaped my mouth that I wish I had never said. "Are you going to be ok after I am gone?" he asked.

## October 24, 2010

Some days it just doesn't seem real, but today I look at his skeleton, his dark sunken eyes. I watch his every move in slow motion, and I realize he's leaving us. One day I will no longer be able to see, touch, hear, or smell him. It's going to be so quiet and *lonely when he's gone. I don't understand why all he has is twenty years. It hurts to know he'll never get married, have children, travel, snowboard, have a career. All this is temporary stuff and doesn't even compare to eternal life in heaven, but still I feel he's been cheated. I'm not blaming God. In fact, He is my rock. He is my strength and hope. I can't imagine trying to go through all of this without my Lord and Savior (Psalm 46:1).*

## MOUNTAINS AND VALLEYS

### Valley

After blowing out the twenty candles on his pineapple upside-down cake, Jedd decided to cut off all communication with his friends and family other than his sister, his nephew, his father, and me. (He did allow occasional visits from his Young Life leader. I learned later that Jedd had committed himself to the Lord at a Young Life camp but began questioning his faith in times of trouble and walked away.)

Although heartbreaking and difficult to respect his wishes, we did so, nonetheless. He loved his friends dearly, and I truly believe he acted in love, not wanting them to witness him wither away, which he seemed to be doing quite quickly.

Hospice increased his pain meds and, like it or not, I was learning to be a nurse—something I never desired to be (that or a dentist – *yuck*). Once in the evening and again each morning I filled the syringe and carefully injected it directly into Jedd's abdomen, alternating between the left and the right sides. The injections helped alleviate some of the nausea and pain. I learned very quickly not to bring my phone during these times. The startling ring-a-ding-ding was not a pleasant experience for either of us when there's a needle in hand.

A small brass bell sat on the side table next to Jedd's chair so he could alert me when he needed me. His voice was barely audible and sometimes hard to understand. Between long naps, he sipped on diluted banana smoothies. Due to severe constipation, pain, and nausea, he pretty much gave up on solid foods. *Lord, I can't believe I'm really going to lose him. It doesn't seem real. I do find comfort knowing that he will be with you forever in heaven.*

**Mountain**

"Mom, I would really like you and Laurae to baptize me," Jedd whispered one day. *What!* A balloon of joy welled up inside of me. *Really? Can I do that at home?* I wasn't sure if we had that authority, but I decided to make some phone calls and find out. Yoo-hoo and glory hallelujah! As Jedd stood partially naked on bath towels laid out on the floor as rugs, one hand gripping the towel rack for balance and the other placed in both of ours, Laurae and I poured a large cup of warm water over his head. Through nervous giggles and what felt like a stumbled prayer, we baptized him right there in our tiny bathroom. What a beautiful moment.

**Mountain Top**

I prayed. I waited. I watched.

*Is this normal? Do people on their deathbed suddenly wake up one morning, have a normal bowel movement after weeks of not having one, ask for food, and start reminiscing on the good ole days? What is happening?* We knew that nothing is impossible with God (Luke 1:37, Matthew

19:26), but we still were unsure if God was answering our prayers for miraculous healing. If so, Jedd wanted to use his testimony to help people with depression, anxiety, and addictions.

I called hospice so many times they knew my voice immediately—even the on-call nurses on duty for the midnight shift. One nurse told me, "Yes, it is sometimes normal for patients to have a surge of energy and alertness, to make final arrangements, make amends with family and friends, a day or two before passing away—a nesting period of sorts. It is possible it could last three days to a week, so enjoy every minute of it."

Three days passed. A week. Then, ten days later, when Laurae came for a visit, Jedd decided he wanted to go out and do something. *Is it safe for him to go out? He's so weak!* Again, I called hospice. "If he feels up to it," they replied. *Oh dear.* He was no longer white, bald, and puffy from the chemo. Instead, he looked ashen gray with deep dark pockets around bulging eyeballs, skin clinging to bone and sinew (except for his swollen calves and feet), a perfect picture of the walking dead. Ghastly.

Dressed in blue and gray flannel pajama pants, a winter coat, a beanie, and size thirteen men's slippers with the sides cut to accommodate his grotesquely swollen lower extremities (so swollen in fact that open sores oozed enough fluid to soak a bath towel within a couple hours. Yes, it was gross!) Jedd made his way to the car while I tried to hold him steady. First stop of all places was Smoker Friendly, a local tobacco shop that carried a myriad of paraphernalia. Although he wasn't really smoking any more, Jedd loaded up on loose tobacco and papers. He said it would give him something to do while he just sat around. I could only imagine what the employees must have thought as I had to help him stand upright after leaning over to examine the merchandise. "The last thing this kid needs is nicotine." Or "Who in their right mind would bring their son out looking like that?" Or "What the ____!"

Next stop, the local grocery market. Customers dropped their jaws as they turned their heads the other direction or stood paralyzed in their tracks at the sight of him. I was accustomed to the way he looked but to see the reaction of others confirmed how horrible the reality of it was. Jedd ignored them all as he and Laurae shuffled through the aisles looking for choice items: crab and wasabi sauce, chili, chicken and dumplings, cheesecake, a candy bar. *I know he wants to eat but should he really be considering all of this? Oh, my goodness. Lord is he getting better or am I just hoping for something that is not real?*

Over the next couple weeks, we enjoyed an outing every day: fishing, late night drives to the hills to stargaze, out for coffee, and back to the grocery store to satisfy the strange food cravings. Jedd's diet would've given any healthy person a bellyache. Miraculously, he no longer suffered from constipation. We even made it to church a couple times. What an exciting and crazy time. If I had not been living it, I would not have believed it was happening. Hospice couldn't explain it either.

## THANKSGIVING 2010

We got a relatively small turkey. With the four of us, there was no need to spend all day cooking a twenty-pounder. Laurae and my husband both brought a favorite prepared dish to set on the meagerly decorated table. Unfortunately, Jedd woke up with some severe back pain that particular Thanksgiving Day and didn't feel like eating. Even the smell made him feel nauseas.

Despite the situation, I talked Jedd into taking a family photo before he headed back to bed. Normally I did not take pictures of him at that time, mainly because he didn't want me to. For some reason, though, this time I could not let the urge go; I begged, and he finally agreed. I am so thankful I did. It is the only picture I have of the four of us, plus my precious grandson Syris.

**Valley**

Hope wavered as nausea, anxiety, sleep, and pain management slowly increased. Seriously, I kept a ledger to keep track of the thirty-two pills and the times and doses each one needed to be given throughout the day and night. By now I was sleeping on the floor next to Jedd's recliner with a timer next to my pillow. Somehow my mind could keep track of medicine but not much of anything else. Eventually Jedd had difficulty swallowing and the number of pills turned into about the same number of syringes I injected into a port in his thigh. I remember filling syringes each morning, checking and checking again the doses and labels. I put the prepared medications in six differently labeled coffee mugs on the top shelf in the fridge. Hospice came every few days, not only to check on Jedd but to check on me too. They said they had never seen anyone run a home ICU like me.

The pharmacists also quickly learned my name and even made special home deliveries for me, which was a tremendous blessing. It was a chore to get out and do errands, and half the time I either forgot where I needed to go and what I went there for. I relied heavily on sticky notes to keep my days and life, such as it was, in order. Jedd would make fun of me. Jokingly he would say, "First, Mom, you need to find the sticky note that tells you where all the other sticky notes are." We always had a good laugh over that one. Otherwise, I just flew on autopilot.

"When you pray for me will you please pray that I don't have to suffer when I die?" Jedd asked early one morning. *He has got to be kidding, I thought. What an amazing young man. He's crippled and in horrible pain from the cancer, his stomach is swollen, he feels sick and weird, and yet he is worried about having to suffer. In my mind he is suffering right now. Lord thank you for the strength, courage, and patience You've already blessed him with. I can't even imagine.*

**Mountain**

*"Merry Christmas, Mom,"* Jedd called out. *"This would be a good day for God to take me, but I don't think He's going to."*

It didn't feel like Christmas time. There was no Christmas music, no lights on the tree, no gingerbread houses, and no excitement.

We all managed to squeeze into Jedd's tiny room, to which he was pretty much confined. Gift-giving seemed pointless in light of the circumstances, but Jedd had special-ordered a ring for Laurae on one of our previous outings. It was a white gold band with each of their birthstones nicely set side by side. He had the words "Love lives forever" engraved on the inside. My heart overflowed with joy that the two of them became so close the last few years. He truly loved his sister more than anyone else on the planet.

# IT'S FINAL

*Wow! I felt like I was blindly trudging through a major snowstorm. At times the flakes were so heavy I couldn't see two feet in front of me. I knew vaguely that things were going on around me, but I couldn't comprehend what they were. I'd look back now and then, and the powder already covered my tracks. With every step I sunk deeper and deeper. I knew I needed to keep moving, but I was tired and needed to rest. Even so, I could not give up. I had to focus and ride out the storm.*

When I felt myself falling, all my strength leaving me, God helped me stand up and carry on.

I wondered how much longer he'd hang in there.

*Oh, how I will miss him, not being able to touch him or hear his voice anymore. It's a shame he can't enjoy the things we take for granted like birds chirping, blue sky and sunshine, but I think of where he will be going and how much better it will be. God's house has many rooms and He is preparing one especially for Jedd (John 14:2). For that I am thankful.*

Laurae, Syris, and my husband stayed the night in anticipation of the inevitable. The waiting was hard. Jedd confirmed all of his wishes with us that he'd prepared months earlier: which of his belongings he wanted each family member or friend to receive, handwritten letters we were to distribute, and a special list of items he wanted Syris to keep when he was older. He made it very clear he wanted his friends to know he died a Christian, and he wanted his Young Life leader to share his sentiments during his funeral.

We found this short poem Jedd wrote during one of his chemo treatments. We didn't know it at the time, but he wrote many poems revealing his thoughts and feelings.

> They've taken my hair,
> They've taken my strength.
> It is not fair.
> But I still have my faith.

*Lord, thank you for the strength, peace, hope, comfort, and perseverance You have provided for all of us. May Jedd continue to feel Your presence and everlasting love. Thank you for holding him in Your arms until forever comes.*

"Jedd, if you can hear me squeeze my hand," I said. There was nothing left I could possibly do for him. Kneeling next to his chair, his bony hand in mine, I prayed. Suddenly, with a burst of strength I didn't know could be possible, he raised his arm high into the air as if reaching for something. His bulging eyes intently scanning the unseen. Then, just as suddenly, his arm fell to his side and his head tilted limply as he exhaled.

I gently laid my ear on his chest. No gurgles, no air, no heartbeat. February 7, 2011, my baby was finally at peace. Be still and know. . . .

* * *

Jedd insisted I not spend the rest of my life searching for a cure for cancer. Instead, I have committed to praying for the salvation of all of his friends so that one day he truly will see all of them again.

# A DYING FRIEND

A letter from a dying friend,
A poem to read at my end.
I'll try and make it true,
'Cuz you need to know I love you.
This one is for all that care.
Just know that I'll always be there.
Live your lives for a reason.
Don't skip-out in an off season.
I ask that you live for love
And take a note from the dove.
Let the world set you free.
I know it's hard but don't mourn me.
Celebrate my death.
Party like you've got nothing left.
Light a big fire and watch it burn.
In the flames there's something to learn.
Soon enough and you'll find peace,
And live your lives with plenty of ease.
Things may get rough,
But all of you are f***ing tough.
In this world there's a lot of sh*t,
So get a shovel and get on with it.
Dig down deep and find yourself.
Do whatever you think will help.
If you only knew what you meant to me,
Your faces are the last thing I'll see.

I may be gone,

But somewhere I'll live on.

This may be my end,

But I'll wait forever to see you again.

This is your letter from a dying friend.

**By Jedd N. Conwell**

*(written approximately eight months before he died)*

# 7

## ||IDENTITY CRISIS||

" **Y**our neck and shoulders are loaded with knots. No wonder you are in pain." Kneading and massaging, the therapist worked me over as my mind wandered. *What will the future bring? What am I to do? Will my marriage ever be restored?* I had not been alone or on my own since right out of high school and the thought of it caused an uncomfortable uneasiness. I tried to pray, but I felt all prayed out.

The mental and emotional whirlwind continued. My mind reeled, spinning, dirt flying in all directions, leaving me in a dust cloud unable to see myself or my surroundings clearly. I struggled with my new identity. I knew who I used to be, but who am I now? I knew who I was when I was a mom, a wife, and a caregiver. What was my purpose now?

The staff and students were extremely patient with me as I re-entered the workplace. My memory and focus were far from par, and I needed frequent reminders. It felt satisfying to be back in the classroom and have a sense of normalcy. I enjoyed being involved with the kids again although I noticed it was getting increasingly difficult for me to get up off the floor and into a standing position. My knees were extremely stiff and achy. At night I would wake up with joint pain in other parts of my body too. What was up with that? Surely, I hadn't neglected myself that much the last six months to create such problems. And I was not old enough for arthritis.

Well, X-rays of my knees revealed mild degenerative joint disease and a spur on the inside of my right knee. Yep, that's where it hurt. *Rugabugs!*

That school year ended and a new one began. The enthusiasm I experienced in the past was not there. Something new stirred inside of me. A shift or change was coming, and I couldn't quite put my finger on it. I truly loved the kiddos and the teacher I worked with, but my heart just wasn't in my work. I prayed that it wasn't obvious to the kids. The feeling never subsided and as that school year came to a close, I sensed God urging me to quit my job.

I looked forward to the summer break, the daily walks or hikes, working in a garden, spending time with Syris, and seeking the Lord's next steps for me. The more I prayed about resigning from my position at the school, the more I sensed God confirming that decision.

"Oh Lord, what is it You would have me do?" I asked aloud on one of my walks. God often spoke to me when I walked alone, enjoying the great outdoors.

"Trust Me. Trust Me. Trust Me," He replied as I perceived it in my heart. That was it. No details, no hints, no glimpses of His future plans for me.

**It didn't matter if I had another job lined up or not.
The point was to trust Him. A leap of faith. He will provide.
It's worldly scary to live with no extra money for rent, food, bills.
The uncertainty was scary.**

I contacted a friend from church who I knew I could trust. I needed to know: Was I nuts? Should I really quit my job when I didn't have a plan? Did I really hear God correctly or am I selfishly wanting a change? I did not have a formal degree, and I was no spring chicken. *Who would want to hire me?* I thought.

"I believe God is calling many of His children into a walk of faith and trust alone," my friend said, giving me examples of Moses and Abraham from the Bible. "God is faithful to His Word," she encouraged me.

I figured two months would be sufficient time for God to reveal what kind of work He wanted me to do before I turned in my notice. In the meantime, people randomly started asking me to house and pet sit. Something I had never done before, nor did I ever mention it to anyone. Turns out it was perfect, flexible, and paid the bills. God truly provided my basic needs such as food, shelter, and clothing. (Matthew 6:25-33). I felt positive, though, that house and pet sitting was not my next career choice. Still, I had no inclination for my future. I half expected jobs to pop out at me while scanning the Help Wanted ads. Didn't happen. I prayed often, but I wasn't hearing anything in my spirit.

Several weeks before school resumed, and still not having a clue what was next for me, I turned in my resignation. Thankfully, the principal understood the call of God on one's life, otherwise I am sure I sounded looney.

It wasn't until I took the step and actually quit my job that God began to show me little bits and pieces of the puzzle. It happened subtly at first, through conversations with people. "You know, I think you should look into Joyce Meyer's ministries," suggested one. "I heard about this one mission organization that you might be interested in," advised another. Ideas for ministry and missions seemed to be the topic of interest that kept popping up. *Oh, my goodness*, I thought. It all came back to me: that one Sunday at church when my body experienced stirring sensations as the pastor spoke of missions. I completely forgot about missions in the midst of all the chaos. *Really?! Missions?!*

"Yes, my dear," that still small voice whispered. I was to share the love of Christ and make Him known to the ends of the earth.

# 8

## LAURAE

While I was caring for Jedd, I had received a dozen hints, and I still didn't get it. "I sometimes feel nauseous in the morning." Laurae told me one day. (She's probably just nervous starting a new school). "I don't like the smell of that." (She always had a very sensitive sense of smell.) "Why all of a sudden do I crave certain foods?" (That I don't know.) "Do you think I have a bladder infection? I have to pee all the time." (She didn't have a fever and didn't complain of pain.) "Mom, my period is a couple weeks late." Laurae's declarations could not have been more obvious. (Well, I was never very regular as a teen either.) *Good grief!*

Finally, while shopping in a Hobby Lobby craft store one day, Laurae announced, "Mom, I'm pregnant." HUH!? Pregnancy was the furthest thing from my mind. By the way, it had only been six months since the car accident that fractured her pelvis.

Abortion was never an option, although some had suggested it. Laurae wanted the child, and I supported her decision, even though it would be difficult. She courageously determined to finish school and go on to college and be the best mom she could.

## PRAYER ANSWERED

As a parent and a born-again Christian, my greatest desire was to see my children walk with the Lord. I had attended several small group Bible studies over the previous year and was currently enrolled in a study on healing and deliverance. I shared with Laurae what I learned each week, not really totally understanding myself how it all worked. Early in January 2010, she asked if she could come along. Not knowing for sure, I called the leader of the group, and he invited her to sit in. And that's what she did, sit in. I glanced at her every so often to see if I could catch a glimpse of any kind of reaction from her, but there was nothing visibly obvious. Afterward the leader spoke with her briefly and then asked her bluntly, "If you were to die tonight, where would you go?"

"I hope I would go to heaven," she answered. The next thing I knew, he walked her through a prayer of forgiveness of others, repentance, and then a prayer of salvation. It was so easy and completely unexpected. I could hardly believe what just happened. My baby, with a baby, was saved and would live for eternity in heaven (Ephesians 2:8-9; John 6:47). Her baptism later outwardly confirmed her commitment to follow Jesus, and her life changed dramatically.

Before we left that meeting, a small group of people prayed for Laurae. One lady in particular, who didn't attend consistently, felt led to lay hands on Laurae's belly and pray for the baby within. At the time, I did not understand the full importance of this gesture. (Keep in mind that God's thoughts and ways are so much higher than ours as he says in Isaiah 55:9).

## PLANNING PERIOD

This was around the time of Jedd's diagnosis, and despite the bad news we all found great joy in the miracle of life that incubated in Laurae's womb. Many of our visits to the hospital included making plans for the baby. We had some good laughs coming up with games for the baby shower. Pin the Umbilical Cord on the Baby brought a few welcomed chuckles.

I wanted to spend as much time with my daughter as possible before she moved into her own apartment. She is my best friend, my crutch and confidant, and I grieved the day she would move out. Her relationship with the baby's father was on again/off again and was an all-consuming strain in the midst of life's circumstances. We prayed and hoped for the best.

Shortly before the baby's birth, Laurae chose to be baptized, and I was honored to be by her side and part of the process. She felt led to share her testimony, and the pastor granted her permission to do so before being submerged. She made my heart sing. *Look at what God has done and is doing in this amazing young lady!* I marveled. Proud mommy!

## GIFT FROM HEAVEN

July 21, 2010, at 12:50 a.m.: "Mom, I think it's time!" Laurae nervously announced over the phone. *Oh, my goodness.* For close to ten hours, we practiced what we had learned in all the Lamaze classes we'd squeezed into our schedule between Jedd's chemo treatments and school. Laurae was determined to deliver her child naturally with no medications. And she did, with absolutely no complications. Not even a broken pelvis could hinder this delivery. Go God!

When we welcomed a beautiful baby boy, Syris Jedd, into the world it was such a blessing. Jedd, holding the newborn, was deeply moved by the fact his nephew would share his name. Grandma cried.

By then, Jedd's debulking surgery was over, hospice came regularly, and we waited at home for the inevitable. We both loved the days when Laurae and Syris came to visit. Babies bring such love and joy. I think Jedd could've just lay next to the baby all day and been content. They held a special and unique bond from the very beginning.

God reminded me how much He loved me through Syris. I loved to hold him, to stare into his beautiful tiny dark eyes, smile at the slightest expressions, caress his tiny fingers, and kiss his sweet little cheeks. It occurred to me then, and I still believe, God desires to hold me in His loving arms in the same way, and to dream of what I will become. He loves me "with an everlasting love" (Jeremiah 31:3).

## MOVING FORWARD

During and after her pregnancy, Laurae attended college and worked on getting her associates degree. We also had appointments with attorneys regarding her settlement from the car accident and another for consultation concerning parental rights and child support. What an ordeal.

After Jedd passed away, we designated Sundays as Stargate Sunday. We ate veggie pizza—not bacon (which was Jedd's favorite)— from Papa Murphy's. Then we settled in and watched an episode of Stargate—the same ones we watched over and over the last couple months with Jedd. We laughed in amazement at how Syris got excited when the theme music played before each episode. It felt good to laugh.

## AMARILLO BOUND

After a spur of the moment decision, we found ourselves on the road to Texas for spring break. It was a time to chill and not think about life for a while. Amarillo was warm, a place we never visited before, and not too far a drive for an eight-month-old sitting in the car seat. We enjoyed a few glorious days soaking up the sun, swimming, strolling through the botanical gardens (my kind of vacation), and participating in the hands-on exhibits at the Discovery Center. We couldn't have asked for something better or more simple.

In the middle of our last night in the hotel, I heard some ruckus outside. Not being too concerned, I rolled over and went back to sleep. How is it when everything seems to be going well you are thrown a curve ball? Or maybe it was a sledgehammer. The next morning, out in the parking lot, we found broken glass everywhere. Our bag of dirty clothes, travel crib, food cooler, and tool bag were missing from the back of the car. *Good grief!* First attorneys and now insurance companies. We were thankful the car was at least still drivable. Most likely the culprits would not be found and what they stole from us and several other cars in the parking lot would never be recovered.

Laurae and I prayed for the thieves, forgave them, and trusted God for the outcome of their actions. Fortunately, we were blessed with warm traveling weather since we drove home with unplanned air conditioning.

## MORE THAN DRAMA

As Laurae continued her education at the community college and pursued her increasingly amazing artistic talent, I was blessed to be able to babysit. It made for some long days since many of her classes were in the evenings, and I worked during the day. Still, I wouldn't have traded it for anything. I cherished every moment with Syris, my sweet little Babycakes.

Being a single mom, Laurae found it close to impossible to have a social life, let alone try to date anyone. The birth father was not dependable and therefore was not a consistent part of their lives. Other young men looked at Laurae as an easy target. Once in the sack, again in the sack, they figured. They wanted her but nothing to do with a child. She was not desperate but desired to have a father figure in Sy's life. *Aren't there any nice stable Christian men out there who would love her and the baby as a package deal and would commit to wait until marriage?*

In fall of 2012, as I finally discovered that God was calling me to do a discipleship training school (DTS) with Youth with a Mission (YWAM), Laurae met a man who many of us believed was the perfect match for her. It seemed like a divine appointment. He was a godly man who wanted to become a pastor, who adored Syris, and who believed God told him Laurae was to be his future wife. They began to spend more and more time together, all three of them. I couldn't have been happier for her and more grateful that she would be in good hands when I would leave town to join YWAM. I blessed the relationship from the get-go.

Sadly, it wasn't long before Broekn N. Evell (a pseudonym) wanted to rush the wedding. He had already squandered Laurae's settlement money from the accident—the money she wanted to put away for college for Syris—on a "family" vacation and on other high-dollar items. "What is yours is mine and what is mine is yours," he told her. He enrolled in a pastoral program in another town close by and was encouraging Laurae to move closer, in the same home. I prayed that their focus always be on God first and that they seek Him in all situations and for all things (Matthew6:33). I prayed that anything that would hinder their relationship with God be removed before they came together as one. *I'm not sure if there's reason for concern or not but there's something I can't quite put my finger on.* A recurring nagging thought troubled me. Believing this union was God ordained, Laurae and I continued to trust that it would work out, despite some of our misgivings.

Communication with family was minimal while I studied and traveled with YWAM. I waited in impatient anticipation to see them again. Oh, how I missed them. Syris turned into a little boy in five short months, and I couldn't wait to make up all the time that seemed lost. I was disappointed to hear Laurae and Broekn's plans changed and that they were planning a move to Florida in August to transfer to a Christian college there. I was more than relieved to discover they decided to wait on the marriage thing. I no longer had peace about that.

Shortly after my return, with a dreadfully heavy heart, we said our goodbyes and they drove away pulling a U-Haul headed to Florida. Thank goodness for texting, as we kept in touch often. Both of their schedules were full and Syris was enrolled in a reputable daycare right next to the campus. At least Laurae could peek in on him throughout the day to see if he was safe, and he loved being with kids his age. It was like an all-day playdate.

Without going into gory details, this romance took a quick turn for the worse. In Florida the world's fastest roller coaster was twisting, turning, making vertical loops, climbing to incredible heights just to drop over the edge leaving a person hanging on for dear life. My daughter and precious grandson were on a ride they didn't want to be on. Laurae would call sobbing, her life in turmoil and poor Babycakes was caught right in the middle of it. Broekn would call me in the middle of the night, confidently rattling off accusation after accusation of the terrible things my daughter had been doing, trying to cover himself and his actions. LIES. I knew they were lies. He clearly played the professional liar well, and I admit a couple times he almost had me convinced. He got angry when I rebuked him, especially if I quoted Scripture to him. Oh, that really ticked him off. The godly man you saw at school, in church, in the grocery store, was definitely not the same man behind closed doors. I feared for Laurae and Syris and rightly so. Hurting people hurt people. How could we have been so blind, so deceived, so naïve? *So stupid.*

With just two weeks left in the term, Laurae and Syris found shelter in a safe house until I could get a plane ticket to go rescue them.

# 9

## |NO MORE HONEY IN THE HONEY POT|

My brilliant idea to escape with Jedd and Laurae to Cañon City had proved totally unhelpful for reconciling my marriage. The longer we were apart, the less we talked, and the less we talked, the further we grew apart. I started to question "until death do you part." We desperately needed a miracle . I can't say I made a huge effort to restore our relationship, even though I prayed. With Jedd's diagnosis and treatments, work, and Laurae's pregnancy, I didn't have the desire or the energy to make it a priority.

Occasionally we met for dinner, but conversation usually centered around the kids. We used to be best friends, lovers, and partners. He wanted the old me, the one he met when I was twenty-one. I no longer resembled that person and did not want to go back. We used to call each other Honey, and it was so sweet.

The morning Jedd passed away my husband and I took a walk, made funeral arrangements, and discussed life. "So, what are going to do now that this is all over?" he asked. "My plan is to finish out the school year and then come home and work on saving the marriage," I replied with very little confidence. He said he was happier now than he'd been and that it would be a good opportunity for me to find myself and do some things I wanted. It didn't sound like an invitation to make amends. *Oh Lord, now what?*

I strongly believed God stated to me, "until death do you part." No matter how I felt about the marriage, I knew it required me to stand firm and trust in His sovereignty. I didn't know how that would look, but the solution appeared hopeless.

"All this Jesus stuff just puts me one step further from you," My husband complained. He was not at all impressed with my decision to go into missions. For the first time, the word *divorce* was mentioned. I think it had been in the recesses of both our minds for a while. It would have to wait, though. I had an opportunity to find myself and move forward.

# 10

## | ON A MISSION TO FIND A MISSION |

"What kind of mission?" I had asked the Lord while hiking Skyline Drive one lovely fall day. Two months had slipped by, and I was no closer to knowing than the day I remembered the initial calling. And I was jobless. *Now what?*

In fall of 2012 after I turned in my resignation and before Laurae moved to Florida I heard that still small voice: "Keep seeking, you will know when you find it." Since nothing seemed obvious, I decided to head to the local library and research the lists of organizations and ministry suggestions I had collected. I did not own a computer by choice and resisted technology whenever possible. Computers frustrated me, and I wasn't looking forward to the headache I was sure I would have when I left the library. Nonetheless, I gave it a shot.

The websites that gave me trouble while navigating I immediately crossed off my list. A couple others looked interesting enough, so I made a note of them and continued my search. One recommended organization was Youth with a Mission, YWAM for short. I wasn't feeling very youthful but what the heck? Once on the home page, which declared YWAM's mission as Knowing God and Making Him Known (boy did that ring a bell), literally the first thing that popped up was: "Are you at a crossroads in your life?" Yep. "Do you feel God is calling you to something, but you don't know what it is?" Oh my gosh, yep. "Then this DTS is for you."—Ok! But what in the world is a DTS?

Further exploration revealed it was a Discipleship Training School and the Crossroads DTS was geared particularly for families and older adults who were at a crossroads in their lives. It couldn't have been more clear. This specific site advertised a YWAM base in Lakeside, Montana. It involved three months of classroom work— the lecture phase—as well as two months on the mission field—the outreach phase. I asked the librarian for assistance to print off some of the material. I would take it home, read it over, and pray about it.

My excitement increased, but before I made a big decision like that I wanted more confirmation. Was this really what God had in mind for me? Like Gideon in the Bible (Judges 6:36-40), I threw out my fleece one more time. Such was my lack of faith.

In the meantime, I had been asked to present a small gift to Pastor John, a missionary who traveled from Uganda, Africa, to visit the Vineyard church. The leaders believed that since I felt like I was being called into missions, it would be appropriate for me to pass on a token of appreciation to the missionary visitor. I agreed—as long as I didn't have to stand up and say anything in front of the congregation. I feared speaking in front of even a small group let alone two hundred church members. Just the thought of it caused the blood to rush out of my head and I would feel like vomiting. My hands would shake, and my knees would tremble to the point of near collapse.

Pastor John had shared his personal story, and part of his message seemed to be speaking directly to me. "When Jesus calls, we go and we don't care whether we are too young or too old or what the world thinks. We cross over to all parts of the world whether our mission is to minister to 1 or 10,000." That was the confirmation I needed.

I remember leaving the church with an odd sense that I would see that pastor again someday. How, where, when, I did not know.

I didn't waste any more time on doubt and turned in all my application forms, letters of reference, a short bio and testimony to the YWAM school in Montana. The months flew by and October arrived before I knew it. The training school started January 3,2013 and I realized I did not have an updated passport and also would need a handful of vaccinations for outreach. Oh yeah, and money! Oh my! I found myself taken right out of my comfort zone and knew this was probably just the beginning. To take on an adventure like this by myself just didn't make sense. What was I getting myself into?

## UNEXPECTED INTERRUPTION

The day after Halloween, the year before moving to Florida, Laurae, Syris, Broekn, and a couple of Laurae's friends helped me move a truckload of my belongings from my place in Canon back to Westcliffe for storage while I prepared to leave for DTS. My daughter also wanted her father to meet Broekn, her new boyfriend at the time. We called and left a message notifying him of our upcoming visit. When we arrived, only the dog greeted us. We weren't surprised by this at first, but after a couple hours and not even a phone response, we became concerned. My husband often showed up late but to not show up at all or to not answer within a reasonable amount of time left us wondering what might have happened.

Emergency rooms and neuro-trauma intensive care units aren't my favorite places to visit. The room reeked of the dregs of the party from the night before. I tried to hold my breath as I leaned over to kiss my husband's forehead and pray a quick prayer over him. With his eyes slightly open but heavily sedated, I'm not sure he acknowledged my presence. His injuries were quite serious, and doctors were waiting on the scans to reveal the results from the trauma to his head, back, and arm. Miraculously, he did not suffer any brain damage or internal injuries when his truck ran off the road and into a berm. It had flipped and rolled before coming to a stop a good distance from the highway. Only by God's grace and mercy did he survive the accident. Thankfully, no one else was in the vehicle and no other cars were involved. He looked a miserable mess, and I felt bad for what happened and the pain he was suffering. Secretly and selfishly, though, I feared I would have to take care of him and miss my DTS. Just being honest. As it turned out, his neighbors were happy to let him stay in their home, drive him to appointments, and let him recover until he was able to care for himself. What a blessing.

As of the first week of November, YWAM Lakeside officially accepted my application for DTS. As I prayed one morning, again wondering if I was on the right track with this mission thing, I felt like God said, "It is a good detour." *Hmmm. Detours sometimes let us see things we normally wouldn't see. I picture a detour where the main road is closed, and there is no other road. This isn't a detour made by choice.*

*OK Lord, show me, teach me, mold me, grow me into Your likeness on this detour. I'm ready to jump, I'm ready to fly for the first time.* I had not experienced so much enthusiasm for who knows how long.

As I made my list and checked it twice for all the things I should and could take (items were limited due to space and sharing a room with multiple other students), I wondered if it would all fit into one suitcase. Winter clothes are bulky and heavy. Then came the phone call from the office in Lakeside: "I am so sorry, but we are going to have to postpone the DTS until April due to a lack of students. If you are interested, the YWAM bases in Chico, California, and Kona, Hawaii, are both offering Crossroads in January. I would be happy to transfer your application and deposits to either school. You will have to make a decision within ten days as it is already now just a month away."

Maybe I didn't hear God correctly or maybe the timing wasn't right. Disappointed but not giving up, I called the school in Chico. The curriculum sounded almost identical to that in Lakeside, but something told me, "not this one." I was reluctant to contact the University of the Nations in Kona. The school fees were a bit more expensive, plus I would have to purchase plane tickets, another unexpected expense. I resolved to wait until April.

However, while walking a couple days later, not really thinking about anything in particular, I heard, "I want you to go to Hawaii. I want to bless you." I literally stopped mid-step in awe at what I had just perceived in my heart. *What? Really? How?!* Suddenly, I was overwhelmed with the urgency to get my paperwork transferred and to check on air fares and availability. I would have to repack, trading hats, gloves, coats, and boots for sunscreen, swimsuit, sandals, and beach towels. *Could this be real?* I made the necessary phone calls and patiently waited for a response from Kona. Tick tock tick tock.

A week passed, and finally I received a response. "The good news is we have reviewed and prayed over your application and have accepted you for the Crossroads DTS. The bad news is there has been an influx of applications this quarter, and the campus is experiencing a housing shortage. We have put you on a waiting list for a bed." (Already there were ten to twelve people bunking in a room.) "We will let you know as soon as possible if something opens up," the Crossroads leader explained.

Waiting again. Time was running out.

I was jolted out of a deep sleep late on the night of December 20. *Oh no!* My initial thought led me to worry that something happened to Laurae or Syris, but the long-distance number was unfamiliar. For some reason I chose to answer anyway. "Holly? This is the leader of the Crossroads DTS in Kona. We have just come out of a meeting. We have beds for you and the other thirty-nine students on the list." I could almost picture her jumping up and down.

"I know it is late, but I couldn't wait to call you." This lady had a grin from ear to ear. I could hear it in her voice. The joy flowed through the phone like rain in a downspout. I could hardly wait to meet her in person.

"You can purchase your plane tickets to arrive no later than January 3. Someone will meet you at the airport," were her final instructions before ending the call.

I couldn't sleep. I was going to Hawaii in less than two weeks. *Wow God, this is some kind of a detour.*

# 11

## CROSSROADS

### ALOHA

Although I was unaware where my bed was going to be, I envisioned a cot in the boiler room or on a bunk in a dorm with fifteen other students. After a thorough tour of the YWAM campus, we took a cruise down Alii Drive, presumably to show me around the area and the views of the ocean. The reality of living on a beautiful island for the next three months began to sink in, and I could hardly hold back the tears. The welcoming, sweet aroma of plumeria trees filled the humid air as it would again later when I was even further from home. The warm sun soaked my body in a way I'd never felt in Colorado. Waves gently washed against the shore as I took in all the new sights and sounds. *Absolutely glorious.*

Surprisingly, my sweet chauffer and tour guide pulled into a hotel directly across the main road that parallels the Pacific Ocean.

They grabbed my suitcase and headed to the front desk. Completely flabbergasted, I followed. This was no boiler room nor was I going to have a dozen roommates. I was blessed beyond measure to have one beautiful Kenyan roommate, a private bath, room service, and breakfast next to the pool. God kept His promise. I lay on the bed and sobbed.

## A VISION

The campus was a lovely milelong walk up the hill to the Crossroads outdoor classroom. I enjoyed the daily exercise after sitting much of the day, although my knee complained and let me know often.

The Crossroads school itself accepted over fifty students and therefore we would be split up when it came time to leave on outreach. Half of the group would go to India, the other half to Israel for five weeks and then we would switch. *India! Israel!*

In one small group session God showed me three things, as I sought a word or a vision concerning our outreach. It was so cool. I never really thought about asking God for a vision about something in particular. I thought He just gave it to you when He was ready. I had so much to learn.

*The first thing I saw was a large open space in what seemed to be a central location within a town. Streamers of blue-and-white triangular flags decorated the area as if it were a child's birthday. A celebration of sorts.*

*The second vision I saw was of several roads connecting but not really having any direction. The words* unrest, fear, *and* no order *came to me. I also sensed that the roads were in a city and a dark cloud filled the sky. I jotted down what I perceived in a notebook, as we were encouraged to do.*

*The third picture I saw was of a hard, desolate area with no vegetation. Sickness, children and some tents or small houses appeared, but so did the sense that God's presence was there. Others in the group received different words or visions. One lady saw a red bike, and that was it.*

## SHIP AHOY

During one of our corporate worship sessions on campus, I received another vision. One so clear I questioned my decision for the Crossroads DTS. On either side of the stage hung two billboard-sized paintings of the ocean. The one to the left displayed the words To Know God, while the one on the right said To Make Him Known. At one point in worship, I glanced up and perceived a big white ship sailing on the waves in the painting to the left. I had heard about a DTS that would be on a mercy ship this quarter. Even though I knew God wanted me at Crossroads, it troubled me, and I wondered if I had signed up for the wrong school. So during the lecture phase when Mark Virkler taught on the four keys of hearing God's voice, I was anxious to ask God what the deal was with the ship. Definitely the most valuable and life changing class for me, and I was so grateful that this teaching preceded all of the rest.

As we practiced quieting ourselves, focusing our eyes on Jesus (usually with light instrumental music in the background), we tuned into spontaneity and began to write down what we heard. I asked the Lord to tell me about the ship. This was His response: *"I want you to float with me into the unknown. Peace, tranquility, beauty, love will overcome you. It's not about the boat, it's about trust and faith. You are my child, and I want the best for you. Sail with me and enjoy my presence—just you and* me." Mark explained that if a message was truly from God, it would reveal His character, and He would confirm it.

I hadn't been in Kona even a month, and already I was missing Laurae and Babycakes something awful. I began to question the relationship she was in and that I had so eagerly blessed from the beginning. Something was off. The second anniversary of Jedd's death drew near, and my thoughts and emotions were all over the place. Not a day went by that I didn't think of him. Still the future of my marriage remained uncertain, and my husband wanted nothing to do with my faith. He said, "people who hear voices need to see a psychiatrist." What to do? It was amazing and heart-warming to be living, studying, and working among such a huge community of believers on fire for the Lord, where there was always someone who cared enough to make themselves available and willing to pray for you.

## JUST HUMOR ME

One requirement for the DTS was to find a local church and attend weekly. I found a small Holy Spirit–filled church just a few blocks from the hotel. No big band worship team, no fancy programs or agendas, no coffee or donuts, only the Word of God and hands-on healing ministry. One particular Sunday a friend of the pastor visited. He had a healing ministry in Colorado. Being a native and wondering if we had any mutual friends, I made a point to introduce myself after the service. After a brief conversation clarifying that we did not share acquaintances, he asked if I needed prayer for anything.

*Well, actually, yes.* My knee still hurt, and the doctors had implied it was arthritic. I informed him that it had been prayed over in the past with no results. I remember him saying specifically, "Just humor me, OK?" He proceeded to inquire what happened and when I first noticed the symptoms and pain. "When I was sleeping on the floor caring for my son," I replied.

"Who was helping you with the caregiving? Did you have any outside support? Where was your husband?" he queried. I told him that basically, I cared for him the majority of the time, doing what needed to be done. He suggested maybe some bitterness and unforgiveness might have taken a foothold in my life. I never blamed anyone for not helping and didn't think I harbored any bitterness toward my family for not being there. He said I had been carrying a heavy burden, and I needed to forgive my husband. He walked me through a time of prayer, and I released my husband into the hands of Jesus and declared it was no longer my burden. *I kid you not, my knee felt like new—no stiffness. I was healed right then and there.* He said bitterness is not from God, so if my knee should start hurting again, I am to tell the enemy to shut up, go away, stop it (Ephesians 4:31 and James 4:7).

## LECTURES AND MORE

In the DTS lectures, I learned that word curses, ungodly soul ties, addictions and generational sins were for real and that I could be delivered from them. My heart could be healed from rejection, abandonment, criticism, judgment, and other deep-rooted issues. I was introduced to teachings on the demonic realm and spiritual warfare. It kind of gave me the heebie-jeebies, but at the same time the subject strangely intrigued me.

The more I learned, the more I wanted to know God on a deeper level. I couldn't get enough and wanted to take advantage of every opportunity. God had so much more in store for me, and I didn't want to miss a thing.

The YWAM campus put on a school fair shortly before our outreaches began. There were secondary schools and volunteer staffing jobs available upon return. I wasn't really sure what I wanted to do after DTS, but I knew I didn't want to go back to an eight-to-five work schedule. Wandering through the fair, I made note of dance, art, and hydroponics schools for Laurae. She had expressed an interest earlier, so I made a point to be on the lookout for her as well as myself. The Bible study school and the school of counseling looked interesting. An Introduction to Primary Health Care school (IPHC) for developing nations caught my eye as I passed by. Oddly, I stepped back, picked up a handout, and stuffed it into my bag. *Not for me.* I already performed all the health care I ever wanted to do with Jedd. Really, I wasn't interested in that myself. *Ugh.* Maybe I was picking it up for someone else. God works in mysterious ways, you know.

# A DREAM

Just as mysterious was a dream I had one night. Only on rare occasions do I remember a dream, let alone have it wake me up. All it was, really, was a book I thought for sure God wanted me to read. I could not relax until I wrote it down:

*Approximately 5 x 7 and ½-inch thick, a beautiful red wine–colored cover with white lettering but no pictures. The title was either Starting Up or Standing Up. I couldn't decipher that for sure. The author's name was not on the book.*

For several days I asked multiple people if they recognized either title with no luck. I resolved to look in the campus library. It appeared to be of great importance that I find this book and read it. Nothing on the shelves. Getting online, I searched and searched. I did find a book titled *Starting Up*, but it had to do with being an entrepreneur. I couldn't see why God would want me to read that. Starting a business was not on my radar. A book *Standing Up* also popped up. As I took a closer look, I concluded that a how-to book on teaching little boys to pee into a toilet was not what God had in mind. I would have to see what I could find when I got home.

"Maybe you are supposed to write it, Holy." (That's how my roommate pronounced my name.) Now that was hilarious! In high school, I'd either ditched my English writing classes or showed up high, drunk, or both. I had no clue how to write a short story or essay—a paragraph, maybe but not a book.

# 12

## ISRAEL

Shortly after midnight, after a long series of flights, we landed in Tel Aviv where we boarded a bus for a three-hour ride to an undisclosed destination. Our twenty-five-member team was too large and noticeable for all of us to stay in one location, so we were split once again. While one team went to minister to Ethiopian refugees in a city not far away, the rest of us stayed and sought the Lord, asking what He would have us do in this area where it was highly frowned upon to share our faith and against the law to evangelize with anyone under eighteen.

It took us a few days to scout out the area by foot as personal transportation was not provided. I was so glad my knee was healed given all the walking we were doing. I was pleasantly surprised to see the little mall area with a central outdoor courtyard decorated with blue-and-white Israeli flags and streamers everywhere. How was I to know back in Kona that we would be in Israel when their country celebrated sixty-five years of independence? There must have been thousands of them strategically placed throughout the city. And if that wasn't a crazy enough reminder that God wants to build our faith by revealing stuff to us in a vision, He wanted to make sure we didn't think it was a coincidence by showing us a lone red bicycle leaning against the fence near the entrance to our accommodations. *How great is our God!*

One afternoon, during a team meeting we became aware of a strange dark cloud covering the city. It came in suddenly and looked like pollution, but there were no factories nearby. It didn't smell, and I don't think there was a fire. It seemed too low and heavy for a cloud. Again, my vision from Kona was validated. After some investigation we learned it was a common occurrence to see dark clouds in the area that time of year. They were the result of major dust storms in the Sinai Desert. *Wow!*

Our ministry involved mostly service-oriented work alongside an established Christian organization that took on the role as a distribution center for Jewish immigrants returning to their homeland of Israel. We packaged bedding, kitchen supplies, and non-perishable food items and shelved them for distribution. Their building needed some fresh paint and minor upgrades and cleaning, so we did that as well. We helped sort out piles of donated clothes and items in a large empty building and pulled weeds at another. When we ran out of things to do, we spent time prayer walking and seeking people or businesses to bless.

I felt honored and blessed one day to be invited to go on an all-day delivery run in the countryside and see sights off the beaten path: rolling hills with olive orchards, banana plantations, pomegranates, corn fields, herbs and flowers. Gorgeous. "We call this bali-gon, which means something like a circus," explained the driver in reference to the roundabouts that seemed to be everywhere. That confirmed my Kona vision of roads connecting but not really having direction. Streets were not on grids like in many cities in the west. On my all-day adventure I was treated to another meal of hummus! While other people were dreading the thought of more hummus, I relished every last bite. Fava bean hummus was my favorite. I loved the local cuisine.

You can't go to Israel without going to Jerusalem, Masada, the Dead Sea, Capernaum, and the Sea of Galilee. I tried to imagine what it might have been like two thousand years ago. I wondered if I could be walking on the same soil as Jesus once did. Never in my life did I dream I would be visiting the Holy Land. Africa yes, Israel no. God was blessing me in ways I could never have imagined possible.

# 13

## INDIA

For a small-town Colorado girl who never traveled much, I was in for jaw-dropping culture shock. All the pictures I had examined over and over in *National Geographic* sprang to life: the brightly colored women's dress, the makeshift street corner shrines, the large, magnificent places of worship where gifts were offered to the thousands (if not millions) of gods, the poverty, the lei-adorned sacred cows, and colorful buildings. The naked children, buses, highly decorated trucks carrying people or produce, vans, rickshaws, bicycles, motorcycles, dogs, pedestrians, cows, all shared the road, the traffic, the trash—all of it just like I saw in the photos.

## MINISTRY

Bangalore, a city of nine million, would be our home and location of ministry for the next month. Unlike in Israel, our days were crammed full from 7a.m. to sometimes 10 or 11 p.m. seven days a week with an occasional day off.

Imagine trying to run a vacation bible school for kids who don't speak English in an unairconditioned three-car garage–sized room with fifty to eighty children ranging in ages from two to seventeen years for four hours every morning. Lots of singing, dancing, games, crafts, and smelly sweat-drenched clothes. (Five-minute bucket baths aren't as effective as showers but when that is all you have, it sure feels good at the end of the day.) The kids' behavior impressed me as did the way the older kids naturally cared for the younger ones, whether they were related or not. It is truly a family-oriented culture where it takes a village to raise a child.

We spent our afternoons visiting hospitals, nursing homes, or orphanages, sharing the love of Jesus and being a helping hand where we could. From there we went to the squatter's slum villages for "house" visits.

When I first heard about doing house visits, I cringed. The thought of going door to door with a gospel tract and asking to share my faith was way out of my comfort zone, and I honestly did not want to be a part of it. As it turned out, that became the highlight of my day, and I looked forward to spending the evenings sitting on a mat on the dirt floor of people's one-room so-called homes. Most of them had no furniture and only a couple personal items. None had running water. Their dwellings barely left enough space for the family of six or more to lay side by side on the floor. They welcomed us with open arms and sometimes offered us a biscuit and Orange Fanta soda. (To this day I don't know where they got it or how they paid for it).

Packed like sardines, with odors just as strong, we shared stories and testimonies and prayed for one another. I say we, but very rarely did I speak up myself. Being the shy introvert that I am, I struggled, wondering if what I might say could really be of any significance. I knew at some point, though, I would have to get over that. *After all, isn't that the reason I'm here?* I thought. *God hadn't called me this far to be a bystander. No, I am meant to stand and testify and share the love of Jesus.*

Well, that day came sooner than I wanted. On Sundays, we attended local Indian churches, some large and some small, and always the men were on one side and the women on the other. The local churches expected us to be ready to share a message or a short testimony at any given service, if we were asked. I secretly hoped I wouldn't have to, but I did have something I felt God wanted me to share if the opportunity arose.

One Sunday in particular, I really sensed my time had come. I couldn't eat and already felt the anxiety twisting my insides. We went to church. Yes, they wanted to hear from the YWAM visitors. *Oh, UGH!* One team member spoke and then another. One more stood up and gave a short message. I just knew I was going to pee my pants and then . . . the local pastor took over and finished the service. *Whew!* Off the hook—or so I thought.

We had never been to a second church service on Sundays, but this Sunday we went to an evening gathering. My heart pounded like a bass drum in my chest, the cheat sheet in my hand made a racket, and as if natural perspiration wasn't enough in the stifling heat, I felt like I was sweating way more than usual. It was my turn. It would have been willful disobedience to refuse to stand up and step to the front of the room. I turned to the ladies next to me and asked them to pray for me.

It was hard enough to keep my thoughts organized, but when I had to wait for the interpreter to translate every couple sentences I wasn't sure I'd make it through without passing out. By the grace of God, I remained standing. I survived—even without relying on my notes—and had a new sense of confidence and excitement that blew me away. I learned at that moment "I can do all things through him who strengthens me" (Philippians 4:13).

## NEW ARK MISSION OF INDIA

Each day of our India ministry, a couple people stayed back for 'house duty.' This position involved fasting, praying for those on outreach and cooking and cleaning for the forty or so people who ate and slept in the same house. It entailed a full day's work, so usually there were no outside ministry opportunities for the ones serving that day. My turn rolled around every seven or eight days.

One particular evening, after my work was finished, the team leader invited me to go somewhere with a handful of people for a short visit. (Visits in India are not typically short.) Exhausted from the house duties, it would have been easy for me to decline, but I didn't want to miss any opportunity and then to regret later not going.

Wow! I was incredibly glad I chose to tag along! Sitting with the founder of New Ark Missions and Home of Hope, we listened as Auto Raja told his story of being homeless, starving, and near death as a child and then how someone rescued him off the streets. Auto desired to do the same for the dying and the destitute who found themselves living on the street, involuntarily or not. The videos he recorded were quite graphic and showed the dire conditions of the individuals when rescued. They had maggot-infested wounds, infections, untreated tumors and growths. They were suffering from starvation, addictions, missing limbs or limbs that needed amputation. All these unfortunates were literally picked up and brought to the Home of Hope to be nursed back to health. Many died, many more recovered, and some stayed, committed to helping the next person brought in. At that specific time there were four hundred fifty men, women, and children living there and recovering.

Deep in my heart, I felt drawn to be a part of that kind of ministry. On the drive back to our house, I inquired about returning. "Why would you want to do that? It is depressing. My intent was to introduce you to another type of ministry in India not to have you stay and serve," the team leader replied. After a moment, he added, "Our schedule is full until the end of outreach, but I will see what I can do." Honestly, I thought that since I was only one of three who showed any interest in returning, a second chance seemed unlikely.

A few days before departing India we were given a choice of going shopping on Commercial Street or going back to New Ark Mission. *Yoo hoo!* I was happy to pass on the shopping any day. Being herded in and out of stores like cows in a cattle drive to look for something I don't need or even want is not what I considered a grand time. An adventure for sure, but fun? No, thank you. Besides, the only souvenir I cared to have was some Indian curry, masala, and a few other interesting spices to practice my culinary arts. I had found those earlier, along with some *dputas* (prayer shawls) as gifts for family and friends. Count me in for the Home of Hope.

A hundred women or more sat, just sat, on the outdoor concrete foundation under any type of shade they could find while others wandered aimlessly around the courtyard. It was strangely quiet, as if the mute button on the TV had been pressed. A couple of ladies sat together picking "things" out of one another's hair like the monkeys who frequently visit the home. (The monkeys are actually quite destructive and cause serious damage to the roofs.) Missing a leg, one woman scooted around on her bottom, no wheelchairs or crutches as far as I could tell. For three hours, I meandered through the area visiting and praying with the women. Even without knowing their languages, I seemed to be able to communicate and connect in a unique sort of way and hopefully shared the love of Jesus. What an amazing experience. I didn't want it to end.

* * *

Our early morning India ritual of sitting on the roof for devotional time and worship was quickly coming to an end. I was disappointed and close to tears thinking of having to leave this place that had become my home the last month. Although I was extremely anxious to see Laurae and Syris, I almost dreaded going back to Cañon City. I sensed it was no longer my home, but God had not yet shown me where my new home might be. Africa? In my dreams. All I knew for sure after this amazing opportunity, I definitely didn't want a humdrum eight-to-five job. I wanted to do missions and couldn't wait to see what God's plans were for me.

A recurring thought—that I needed ten thousand dollars and to sell all of my belongings—settled deep within my soul.

*Hmmm.*

# 14

## | NO THANK YOU–I'D RATHER NOT |

On Laurae's twenty-first birthday I sat in the airport in Honolulu waiting for my flight back to Colorado. I longed to hug my daughter and my precious Babycakes. Five months seemed like forever to be apart.

My mom had moved to Cañon right before I left, and it looked like I would be staying with her until I figured out where God would send me next. Going back to Westcliffe with my husband wasn't an optimal choice at the time. The gap in our relationship had grown even further apart.

An uncomfortable feeling plagued me that summer as I tried to busy myself waiting for God to show me my next mission. I did not want to be back in Cañon and avoided looking for fulltime work. I did take on some part-time yard work and house and pet sitting jobs. That allowed for plenty of time to reflect, pray, and seek guidance, but it seemed to be getting me nowhere.

Just when you think God has forgotten you, He makes a surprise visit. A slight breeze cooled the perspiration that ran down my back and chest. The mist from the sprinkler was refreshing as I deadheaded spent flowers and pulled weeds in the perennial garden at a house that I was hired to oversee for a couple months. Not a cloud around to filter the intense rays of the sun. Another beautiful day in the life of yard work. With the timer set as a reminder to move the hose, I took cover on the porch, pulled out my journal, and began to write.

Suddenly, swarms of small pesky flies invaded my space. They tickled every inch of bare skin as the little buggers searched for a remnant of water still lingering on my flesh. Not a second passed without one buzzing my ear or attacking my eyes. Shooing them away proved unsuccessful. All I wanted was a few minutes alone with my paper and pen. They were driving me bonkers. I just about had it when I caught myself saying out loud, "God, why did you create flies?" Immediately I heard, "To annoy you." *Wait. What?* I could almost hear Him chuckle, and I could not help but laugh myself. God has a sense of humor!

I had to make note of that in my journal. That cracked me up. What happened next amazed me even more than a holy sense of humor. Lifting my pen and looking out over the yard where the sprinklers refreshed the dry grass, I noticed the swarm of flies that just about ruined my day were now within an arm's length away. They were still present. I could see them clearly, but not a single one of them landed on me or bombed my face. Even after I got up and changed the water and came back with a fresh residue of moisture on my body, not a lone winged pest came close. Forty minutes passed while a mass of black flies hovered at a distance. I kid you not.

I received a personal revelation that afternoon that God pays attention to every detail of our lives. If He cares about pesky flies and removes them when I didn't even ask Him to, how much more did He care for the bigger issues and concerns in my life? (1 Peter 5:7). Do I look for a job? Do I wait? What about my marriage? Why was I feeling so uncomfortable?

August came, and I still had no leads for jobs or possible mission opportunities. In prayer, I wrote what I sensed God was speaking to me:

*My dear child, I will bring work to you. Don't worry about the amount of money or the specifics of the job or the job itself. I would like you to stay in Cañon for a while—a short while.*

My idea of short and His idea of short concerned me.

My friends and coworkers reported back to school in anticipation of the new year a week or so before the children would walk through the doors. I figured if I stepped in before the kids, I would have a pretty good chance of saying hello to most of the staff. A staff meeting was just wrapping up, and I was invited to sit and wait until they finished. It was lovely and relaxing to be sitting there and not be an active participant in preparation for the upcoming academic year.

"It is interesting that you showed up today," the principal said as I headed toward the library where the staff gathered. "The woman who took your place last year turned in her resignation last night. Would you be interested in having your job back?" she asked.

*NO! Absolutely not!* God had bigger and better plans for me, I knew that for sure. I replied politely, "No thank you, but I will pray about it." *Ugh, now why did I say that?* It came out without thinking, just like when I told the sweet little girl I would go to her church at the Vineyard. I did not want my old job back. No more eight-to-five employment for me.

I prayed. When you ask God for guidance and He repeatedly speaks directly to your heart you better be prepared to follow through in obedience. I wanted to hear a no but that wasn't the case.

Yes, He wanted me to accept the job that He brought to me, and I had this uncomfortable feeling that it looked like a two-year commitment. Not a happy camper! I'm pretty sure I cried and threw a holy temper tantrum. Someone once said that disappointment sometimes equals His-appointment. We'll see. I reported to work the next week, assigned to the first-grade classroom.

I didn't mind zipping jackets, peeling oranges, fixing ponytails, and wiping snotty noses or "end of the world" tears. My heart ached when the children's were broken. I felt their crushed spirits when ugly words were spoken to them. I experienced their joy when they found the long-lost favorite eraser. I jumped in excitement with one little boy missing his two front teeth announced, "There's a pider in my wocker; there's a pider in my wocker!" Sure enough, there was a spider in his locker. I truly enjoyed the kiddos but couldn't figure out why I was back in the classroom when God had told me to quit a year ago.

Only He knew.

# 15

## MY HOME THAT IS NO LONGER MY HOME

A nagging desire to have my own place resulted in my renting a nice little one-bedroom duplex with a basement. If God meant for me to be around for a couple of years, I wanted a place to call my home. I love my mom dearly but living with her created a challenge. She had been single way too long and had grown stubborn in her ways. Since she had become more forgetful and confused and found even simple tasks increasingly more difficult, I didn't want to move too far away. She had once been a very social person, but now she mostly stayed home. My duplex was only six blocks away, which made it easy for me to visit any time—plenty close enough for me to keep an eye on her. Selfishly, I looked forward to time alone in my meagerly furnished abode.

That lasted about a month. Little did I know I would be spending my Christmas break going to Florida to rescue my daughter and grandson from the hands of an abusive relationship . We packed up Laurae's few belongings and made the lengthy drive back to Colorado.

A tormenting fear lingered in the back of both our minds that maybe Broekn would try to find them. I was nauseous, heartbroken, and scared for both of them. I prayed fervently and trusted God to make things right.

Thank goodness for the duplex basement. We turned it into a makeshift bedroom for me. I needed to be in Cañon for Laurae "for such a time as this" (Esther 4:14). God knew all along.

## STARTING OVER

"I don't care if I have to raise Syris on my own", Laurae declared matter-of-factly. "I don't want anything to do with a man ever again! The first thing we are going to do is sign up for a self-defense class. I think there's a karate school that teaches adults, children, and toddlers." By golly there was, and she didn't hesitate to register.

Dressed in his mini white karate uniform, Syris maneuvered around the obstacle course in the dojo. Throwing punches, blocking attacks, and kicking foam pads, he ran from station to station. All fun and games for a munchkin with abundant energy. Laurae took it more seriously, as a necessary skill. I enjoyed watching their progress, and I cheered them on.

I sure did like being Grandma and having both of them in the same house. Laurae may tell you differently, but I was truly blessed. Syris became my cooking buddy, and I allowed him to sit on the counter and help. I cherished the mornings when Laurae slept in and Sy would quietly tiptoe to the top of the basement stairs. In his sweet toddler voice, he called, "Gamma, you wake? Gamma, git up. Gamma, make muffins!" Who could resist that?

## A YEAR LIKE NO OTHER

*I'll take you places you've never dreamed of. A journey with me of utmost enjoyment and pleasure. The time is near – closer than you think.*

*This year will be like no other. Don't get discouraged. Know that whatever you face is part of my plan to grow you and conquer. The forces of evil will continue to attack, but they cannot hurt you. Take a stand in Me. Know who you are. You belong to Me not this world (1 John 5:18).*

*Upon a piece of driftwood floats an angel in white, beautiful and caring and lost in a dream. The dream is real but only a glimpse of where she's headed.*

That is a portion of what I journaled as God spoke to me in prayer for that new year. How was I to know the significance of these words as the days rolled by? God is faithful and He knew.

## INVITATION

For years I dreamed of going to Africa. I really don't know when it started or how or why, but I put it on my bucket list before I even knew what a bucket list was. Out of the blue one day in May, while talking to my church friends, the ones who taught the healing and deliverance class I attended, one mentioned going to Uganda and Kenya in August. He traveled there often for ministry but that year his wife would be accompanying him. Would I be interested in joining them? Oh my gosh, yes, yes, yes! Oh Lord, I don't want to pass up this opportunity to do a mission trip. I prayed.

The next thing I knew I was applying for a visa, scheduling appointments for required vaccinations, and wondering how I'd come up with the finances to cover it all. My dream was quickly becoming a reality. I felt like I had just won the Publishers Clearing House Sweepstakes, but this was even better!

## WHO REALLY DOES THIS?

Back at the dojo in late February, a nice-looking young man sporting a black belt approached me after class. I knew him as Sy's instructor, but occasionally he taught the adult classes. I also recognized him as the drummer on the worship team at church. He appeared somewhat nervous. "I'm kind of nervous, and I'm not very good at this," he began. "I was wondering, um, would it be ok if I asked Laurae to coffee?"

I'm sure my jaw must've dropped to my waist. First of all, who asks permission these days to take your daughter to coffee? Secondly, poor guy, no way would Laurae say yes. She had absolutely no interest in dating again after what she had just been through. I felt so bad for him. He mustered up the nerve to ask me, so how could I tell him he was going to be rejected? I thanked him for being a gentleman and appreciated his thoughtfulness. I did not have the heart to say no so a reluctant yes came out.

"Mom, Nathan asked me out for coffee," Laurae said with a hint of excitement in her voice. *Oh dear, here it comes.* "I told him to get lost," is what I expected her to say. No! She actually accepted the invitation. "I'm going to give it to God," she added confidently.

*Lord, if this is not of You in any way, shape, or form, I ask that You slam this door shut ASAP!* I prayed. Oh boy did I pray.

I really liked Nathan, but this time I used extreme caution in blessing any kind of relationship. I did not want to be deceived again and really watched his every move like a hawk. Laurae is an adult, but I am still her Mom. I especially watched how Nathan treated Syris, and how Sy reacted when he spent time with them.

BAM! Four short months went by, and I was at the store looking for a formal dress to wear to an August wedding! You hear of couples falling in love and getting married right away, but I never thought Laurae would be one of them. My initial shock turned to joy and excitement.

As I said before, God works in mysterious ways, and I don't believe there is any such a thing as coincidences in His Kingdom. I had never really put two and two together until the day I realized that a woman from a small group Bible study was Nathan's mom. It turned out that three years earlier, when Laurae was saved in the living room after a healing and deliverance class, the woman who felt led to lay hands on Laurae's belly and pray for the child in the womb was unknowingly praying for her future grandson. When I found out, I knew this was a predestined union. God knew. I cry every time I think of this and how much God loves us, and the great lengths He will go to prove it to us.

## MAMMO-SCHMAMMO

Every year—usually in the spring for me—middle-aged woman get a mammogram. Every year, it's the same routine: in, out, and results within a week. The results are normal, and you check that duty off for another twelve months.

That year, I received the radiology report in the mail as usual, but this time they required a biopsy. I wasn't concerned. Fibrous cysts or calcium deposits are fairly common, plus I have no family history of breast cancer.

A week after the biopsy I received a call to schedule an appointment to go over the results with the doctor. I hate to sit in the waiting room for an hour or more, pay a fifty-dollar office visit fee, then waiting another fifteen to twenty minutes in a small room only to have the physician's assistant tell me, "All is good, and we will see you again next year." I let the receptionist know I didn't intend to make an appointment just to hear that I'm fine.

"I'm sorry ma'am, we can't discuss results over the phone. You will have to meet with your provider," she said apologetically.

*Good grief!* Getting a bit perturbed, I made it clear I would not schedule appointment unless the tests were abnormal. I know she was just following regulations but again she told me she was not at liberty to give any information over the phone. I waited on hold for an annoying fifteen minutes, and finally a nurse picked up.

"Mrs. Conwell, the biopsy is not normal. It's important you come in." *Double good grief!* I made the appointment for the following week, the last week in June.

"What took you so long to come in? The radiology reports from the biopsy reveals two types of cancer: ductal carcinoma, which is usually slow growing and is confined to the ducts, and comedo necrosis, which is a very aggressive cancer and can spread into the lymphatic system. You should have had a mastectomy yesterday," The physician's assistant reported while pacing the clinic room floor and tapping her clipboard.

How was that for a greeting?

"I have already scheduled an appointment for you with a breast specialist and surgeon. She is one of the best in the state. This is serious," she continued.

"But my daughter is getting married August 8, and two weeks later I have a trip planned to Africa." That was all I could think of to say. I didn't want to miss either one.

"You can't go. You will die." Honestly, that is what she said. I knew in my heart that was a lie from the devil and immediately chose to disregard the comment and not agree with it.

I left the office, called some friends from the car to see if they were available to pray for me. The power of prayer!

While I waited, I tried to keep my daily schedule as normal as possible. July seventh, the day before my surgery, I listened to a new CD by Mercy Me. God used music multiple times to speak to me. If someone had been walking past my apartment that particular afternoon and peered in the window, they probably would have thought *that chick has lost her marbles*. A little more than a middle-aged woman was dancing with her hands raised high above her head, tears streaming down her face, and singing to the song "Flawless" that blared from the speakers. I'm sure it was quite a sight. As I declared out loud that I was flawless, "because the cross was enough," I knew I would be OK, and the cancer would be gone.

**I have so much peace it seems unnatural. Praise be to God. Let us rejoice and be thankful in all circumstances. Greater is He that is in me, than he that is in the world (1 John 4:4).**

The surgery went well, and the biopsies of several lymph nodes revealed the cancer had not yet entered my lymphatic system. As a precautionary measure, the doctor suggested I consider six weeks of radiation treatments, just in case. I chose to forego any treatment, believing I truly was flawless and cancer-free. (To this day I am cancer-free!) The best news overall—I was cleared to go to Africa as long as I could regain full range of motion in my left arm. Yoo hoo!

## MY ANGEL IN WHITE

Nestled in a grassy nook,
Bordered by a bubbling brook,
What a sight, my angel in white.
Lord, I pray,
Thank you for this glorious day.
Only You could orchestrate something this divine,
For better, for worse this family of thine.
(Laurae and Nathan married.)

## "JAMBO, RAFIKI"

("Hello, friend")

Uganda was not at all what I pictured. I expected wide open plains with elephants and lions sneaking a drink at a lonely oasis. Instead, I found myself in a lush, tropical environment with fields of sugar cane, tea, and banana plantations.

Upon our arrival in Mbale, where we would begin our two-week ministry adventure, we connected with Pastor John. He would be our guide, chauffeur, and leader. This was none other than *the* Pastor John to whom I presented a gift at the Vineyard church two years previously. God is so good and amazing. *Never in a million years!*

If we weren't attending graduations, meeting and sharing at local churches, visiting orphanages, or participating in the evening crusades, we were on the road to the next city or village. Everywhere we traveled a little thought entered my mind: Would this village someday be my home? *Wow! Look at that garden plot. How I would love a garden again. Oh, so beautiful, I think I could live here. How could God use me in a place like this?* I truly expected and anticipated a Holy Spirit moment that would guarantee my next mission assignment. I was in Africa for goodness' sake!

Nothing excited me more than praying for individuals, especially after the crusades. Hordes of people flocked to the front of the crowd, waiting their turn. We could have spent the entire night laying hands on the old, the young, and everyone in between. At a certain given time, we *mazungas* (white people) were ushered out and taken to our accommodations.

I remember one particular crusade where we had the privilege of being the guests of honor. We were invited on stage, and the program directors wouldn't take no for an answer. Believe me, I tried. We anxiously wondered why we were asked to approach the platform. The stage itself was pretty unstable and adding an extra half dozen people to the already full surface concerned me a bit. On top of that shaky platform, I became a bit unstable myself, looking out at hundreds of beautiful, dark-skinned faces waiting in anticipation for the *mazunga* guests to perform.

If I had known we were going to dance, I would've called in sick. I used to love to dance, especially after a few drinks. But that was the old me. Africans, on the other hand, can dance. There's no doubt in my mind they came out of the womb dancing to the beat of a drum. The music began, I put an artificial smile on my face, and started movin' and groovin' the best I could. One arm swinging here and there, the other close to my ribs as if in an invisible sling, still healing from surgery, I did not have full range of motion yet. Bad patient!

One point that struck me to the core about the African people was their faith and gratitude. I hate to admit it, but I got tired of them saying "praise God" for every little gesture or blessing. I groaned, *enough already!* But in reality, they meant it from the bottom of their hearts. Fresh water, a meal—whether they enjoyed one or three a day or, perhaps, a week—a sunny sky, a rain shower, shoes for their feet, education for their children, or a safe place to lay their head at night. These luxuries were not taken for granted like they often are in the west. They sincerely praised and thanked God for all He provided. They lived day to day in faith. I was humbled and convicted.

Before I knew it our busy fourteen-day mission trip came to an end, and I boarded an international flight headed home without any promise of returning.

**"Continue to follow Me, and I will show you things you could never imagine and what most people will never see." God speaks.**

## A TICKET TO TARSHISH

My job and the precious students welcomed me to the first-grade classroom immediately upon my return to Cañon City from my trip to Africa. Precious little souls with brains like sponges, hands ready to build and create, and hearts seeking love, acceptance, and affirmation that they are unique and beautiful individuals had already been in the classroom a week when I returned from Uganda.

There is power in the tongue, and I had experienced that first hand over the years. It's painful and cuts deep. Our words can either build up or break down the self-esteem and spirit of an individual. Words can be life giving or life draining (Proverbs 18:21, Ephesians 4:29). It grieved me to hear ugly words spoken over a child, even if it was meant as a joke. A crushed spirit broke my heart, and I could no longer stay silent. My good intentions backfired.

I have to say that my final year at the school proved to be an extremely difficult one for me for reasons I choose not to disclose. Like Jonah, when God asked him to go to Nineveh, I wanted to purchase the first ticket on the ship to Tarshish and travel the total opposite direction. I was tempted to call it quits more than once, but I knew God wanted me in Cañon at least one more year. Standing in the strength of the Lord, I made every effort to finish strong. Each time I complained and threw a "poor me" pity party, He reminded me of the blessings and miracles He had performed the previous year—restored hope for Laurae; a wedding; a long-awaited, dream-come-true trip to Africa; and a job with insurance that helped cover medical bills that otherwise would've been out of pocket. Not to mention a body free from cancer. My God loved me with an everlasting love, and He knew exactly where I needed to be at the perfect time. Cañon was my home that was no longer my home, and I chose to stay until He told me to move.

Rejoice always. Pray without ceasing. Be thankful in all circumstances for that is the will of God in your life (1 Thessalonians 5:16-17).

Easier said than done.

## UNTIL DEATH DO YOU PART

It had been almost seven years since my great escape, when Jedd, Laurae and I left our home in Westcliffe. Prayers for a reconciled marriage seemed to have failed. I shared the probability of divorce with a prayer partner, as well as my feelings of guilt for not putting more effort into the restoration process. I felt like I had disappointed God and was being disobedient to what He had told me. I was 99.9 percent sure God had said, "until death do you part." I didn't understand that, and I couldn't reconcile it with what was happening now with my marriage.

Looking directly into my eyes, my prayer partner declared, "But Holly, there *was* a death."

* * *

*It was so true.* At that moment, a heavy weight lifted off my shoulders.

The very morning that Jedd left this world my husband expressed how much happier he was alone, how it was time for me to find myself and move forward. It is never God's divine design for marriage to end in divorce. But it happened.

## INTRODUCTION TO PRIMARY HEALTH CARE?!

*Father, I am sensing some changes coming. You said there would be and I'm excited to see what You are doing.*

Of all the things God could have put on my heart, he chose that little flyer that I had stuffed into my bag at the YWAM school fair. Didn't He know that becoming a nurse or dentist was at the very bottom of the list of my career choices?! *Yuck!* I had already performed more than my share of nursing with Jedd and had absolutely no desire for more.

Ignoring it didn't help. Pretending it was someone other than God speaking didn't help. Throwing away the flyer didn't help. *Rugabugs!* I was going to have to choose to be obedient despite my feelings.

When I asked God to use me for His Kingdom and agreed to do whatever He might ask and really meant it, there was a huge expectation involved. I should expect God to answer and give me opportunities to be His hands, feet, and mouthpiece in the world. When He gives me promptings and opens doors of opportunity, He expects me to stand up, do my part, and follow Him.

A pastor once said, "You don't have to understand fully to obey immediately and completely." God may take you way out of your comfort zone, give you a dream that appears financially impossible, or, as in my case, an assignment that is not very appealing. Then what? If you know it's from God, you do it anyway.

Back to the library I went to research mission organizations that offered health care training. IRIS, a branch of Heidi Baker's ministry in Africa, sounded stimulating. Especially the supernatural healings that took place there on a regular basis. But somehow I kept coming back to Introduction to Primary Health Care (IPHC) schools within YWAM. Several bases in different parts of the world offered the six-month intensive course. The school in South Africa remained on the continent for their outreach. That was appealing and *I* was really leaning on applying for that school. *I* wanted to go back to Africa and thought that since *I* always had an interest in Africa that God was going to send me back there. But such was not the case. God seemed to think Australia was the place for me.

Australia, Australia, Australia. All of a sudden, I was seeing and hearing Australia everywhere.

One morning, as I walked along the ridge of Skyline Drive that overlooks Cañon City, I could hear the faint sound of music and the thump thump of drums. *The high-school marching band must be out practicing*, I thought, although I could see the school from the ridge and there was no band, no people at all, for that matter. I didn't recall seeing announcements in the paper for a weekend concert in one of the parks. The music became louder and the words clearer. *Christian music! That's odd!*

> "I'll stand with arms high and heart abandoned
> in awe of the one who gave it all."

As the song continues it suggests I am completely His, surrendering and offering my heart to God and God alone. The music and the lyrics were as clear as could be. Then, as suddenly as it had started, it was over. No more music, nothing. The band that performs that song is from Australia.

I realized that day the life I chose to live was no longer my own but Christ who lives in me (Galatians 2:20), and I must move forward into the IPHC training for developing countries in Australia, not Africa.

Two of my biggest questions were: Why primary health care? And Why me? The divine answer I received was: *The skills I will learn in primary health care is my ticket to get into the places (plural) God wants me to go.*

Lyrics from another song grabbed a hold of me, and saline waterfalls poured down my cheeks:

"Take me deeper than my feet could ever wander;
and to go wherever You may call me."

*Oh my,* the uncomfortable excitement and uncertainty of the future was a bit much. *"Oh Lord, where are You taking me?"* I wondered. An unexpected response: "OUT ON THE WATER, SILLY." It was a darn good thing God didn't tell me that was literal as well as spiritual.

Once I had surrendered, I had a sudden urgency to purge myself of all my belongings and to get myself into top physical condition. I knew I was not in very good shape and the year before I had sensed a prompting to take it seriously, but I hadn't. Little did I know that part of IPHC outreach would be trekking through the jungles of Papua New Guinea bringing health care to remote villages. *Oh dear!* Three months before boarding a plane I signed up for a fitness and strength training class and went faithfully five days a week.

In early September I drafted and finalized my fundraising letter. Back when I was in India I had a funny feeling I was going to need ten thousand dollars sometime in the future. When I calculated all of my expenses together—I dreaded asking people for money—I found that I needed an estimated total of (you guessed it) ten thousand dollars. I had four months to come up with the money from the day I mailed pleas for help and started speaking to others whom I hoped would fund me. It was a humbling experience.

Within three weeks I had miraculously received seventy-five percent of my goal and by the end of two months the entire IPHC fees, flights, and expenses had come in, plus an extra two thousand dollars. Only God!

## THE COST

In a way I was grieving: grieving the end of a marriage, the end of a job with regular income, the loss of a son to an untimely death, the loss of a daughter and grandson to Nathan and the loving hands of Jesus, and, possibly, the loss of the way of living I was accustomed to. Was I willing to give up everything to be with Him? I had to count the cost.

**The Cost:** Leaving family; giving up my possessions; not worrying about a job or finances or what I would eat or wear;

not knowing where I would lay my head; opening myself up to the possibility of persecution—physically, spiritually, emotionally, and mentally. HELP! Knowing that I am not capable, knowledgeable, bold, strong, faithful enough without Him who makes all things possible. Letting go of my earthly identity to be identified by Christ who abides in me. Relying not on my own understanding but on the trust and guidance of the Holy Spirit. To love others more than myself. Knowing that I may be lonely but never alone. Lord I cannot fully comprehend the cost of following you, and I am sure there will be times I wish I was in my comfort zone. Forgive me now. Even so, I want to choose now to be Your good and faithful servant, with whom You are well pleased. I love You Jesus, my Friend, my Comforter, my All in all.

Again, while walking on Skyline, God showed me a vision of myself, arms outstretched, my left hand holding tightly to Jesus' hand while my right hand grasped Laurae's. He told me I could not follow Him if I was still holding onto Laurae. I had to let go and trust Him. I would get to spend eternity with them. That was tough! Really tough! Especially since I was a grandma a second time to a beautiful baby girl, Esther Kira. Oh, my heart.

In the meantime, I had several yard sales and sold pretty much everything I had left. During the divorce, I felt compelled to leave all the furniture and the house with my husband, so I really didn't have that much. I did have a difficult time getting rid of books, especially cookbooks, and my lovely collection of house plants. Most of my kitchen gadgets were packed away for a future life. Why it was such a struggle to part with kitchen stuff and books, I don't know.

I also moved back in with my mom until my departure date. I was quite concerned with her memory. I tried to decipher how much was actual memory loss, stress, and physical pain from a fall she had taken earlier. She refused to seek medical help or testing for dementia and Alzheimer's. Openly, she admitted that she didn't want me to go and joked about who would do the cooking when in reality it was a real concern for her. Very rarely did she prepare a meal anymore, although she could still make an awesome salad. Her checkbook was a disaster, but I wasn't allowed to touch it. It wasn't unusual for her to get lost on the way to the grocery store or doctor's office, either. Many times, I woke up in the wee hours wondering and praying if I should postpone my training in Australia and stay home to care for her. It was heart wrenching to make the decision to proceed and trust God to care for her. I knew it was time to go, and God honored that choice.

## MY SECRET PLACE

Skyline Drive became my outdoor prayer closet and my secret place, a place where I could cry out to God and He would answer. I never knew if I would come home in tears, laughing, in awe at the revelation that was just revealed about His mighty love and character, or with another research topic He impressed upon me. Skyline Drive was the place I looked forward to walking and being alone with my Father, Friend, Guidance Counselor, and Helper. I had many inspirational moments. These are a few of my favorites.

# 1

## BUTTERFLY

A fat green caterpillar inched its way across the narrow dirt path on the side of the hill. As it slowly tried to maneuver itself over a tiny ridge of dirt, I watched as it repeatedly climbed and rolled back again. "HOLLY THAT IS YOU RIGHT NOW," said that still small voice. "BUT SOON YOU WILL BE WRAPPED UP IN MY COCOON WHERE I WILL BE WORKING ON YOU, TRANSFORMING YOU BEFORE I RELEASE YOU."

In grade school we studied the life cycle of a butterfly, but I felt there was a little more to it, so I went back to the library. Plus, I needed a refresher course. I settled on a book specifically about the monarch butterfly. Now, I don't know if this is true of all butterflies, but I was amazed at the design and planning on God's part in the creation of the monarch. Not a single detail was left out. I learned the caterpillar feeds only on the leaves of a milkweed plant. It molts four times as it grows and then takes a long walk to look for a safe place to hang. Once it finds the perfect location, it sheds its skin one last time and a hard case or chrysalis forms around its body. While hanging in the pupae stage, the body of the caterpillar completely breaks down into a green soupy mixture. Within a couple weeks, the chrysalis becomes clearer, and the green juice takes form in the noticeable parts of a butterfly. Soon it will break out of its cocoon. As the new butterfly hangs and dries, liquid from its body is pumped into the veins of the wings. The liquid that now flows through the veins came from the diet of milkweed in the caterpillar stage.

That liquid substance contains a poison that makes birds and other animals sick if they eat it. Through metamorphosis, the caterpillar is completely transformed and now leads a new life. Monarchs are made to spread pollen from one plant to another, creating a foundation for new life while they nourish themselves with the life-giving nectar of the flowers.

I was totally blown away by the correlation of God's transformation of the caterpillar and the transformation of a follower of Jesus:

- Through trials and tribulations God is removing layers of our fleshly worldly nature so that we may grow in the knowledge of our Lord and Savior and become more like Him.

- Sometimes we feel as though we have been hung upside down and confined in a bubble, when in reality God is completely transforming us from the inside out.

- The food we take in, our daily bread and God's Word, runs through our veins and protects us from the enemy.

- When we break through our shell into our new identity, we are free to fly great distances and spread the life-giving good news from one individual to another. The butterfly is created to pollinate the plants and God is responsible for producing the fruit. Just as we are called to plant the seeds of hope and salvation in our neighbors, God is responsible for bringing them to fruition.

My research into the life cycle of the butterfly and the connections I found between it and the spiritual life helped me to look forward to my own transformation and release into this new season of my life.

## 2

## SUNFLOWER

One particular stretch of the trail was blanketed with beautiful wild sunflowers. I was drawn to examine one a bit closer. I noticed that each branch had its own set of blossoms, mature seeds, and empty seed heads. This may all seem trivial or unimportant but as God showed me, *nothing* can survive apart from His divine purpose. For the sunflower, the flowers bloom in God's time, seed heads form—some still full with seeds while others have already fallen or been scattered by the wind and birds or other small animals. Some seeds blow away and never take root, some land and will reproduce, and others are food and nourishment to animals. And all the while the sunflower plant has no idea in itself what God is doing, how He is doing it, when or why He is doing it. The sunflower is His creation and must rely on Him for water to grow into mature plants and multiply. These particular plants are growing in arid hot soil with no shade. They are growing among lots of prickly pear cactus.

We are like these branches, some blooming, some full of seeds, and some where seeds have been nourishment to others while the rest have been planted. We don't know when, how, why, or where each seed will end up. We only know we need to trust God to do the work. Our job is to bear the fruit or seed and release it in God's timing. We are all at different stages of maturity, and God will have some of us living in dry desolate areas among thorns that no one wants to touch, even though we bloom in season and are beautiful. God showed me I cannot work to speed up the maturity process. The outcome of what I do as a branch is not up to me, and I don't have to know or understand what, why, how, or when God is doing something (John 15:5).

# 3

## STORM

In early November I watched dark heavy clouds brewing over the Wet Mountains from the top of Skyline. Thankfully, I was on the last leg of my walk as the rainstorm quickly approached. In awe at the way the sky was moving and changing, I asked the Lord: "What is in a storm?" Before I could even finish the question, the answer came: "POWER."

Wow! There is power in a storm. I thought of the storms in our lives. God's power is right in the middle of it, and we don't see it until the storm has passed. God's glory is found in our storms. His power is released in the storm, His power is in control of the storm (even if it doesn't appear that way at the time), and His power will bring us out of the storm. So simple yet so profound and powerful.

# 4

## ROCK

The dirt trail, just wide enough for a person to walk single file, traversed the rocky hillside below Skyline. This was the umpteenth time I had come around the corner, but never had I seen "the rock." Stopping mid-stride, I peered at the unusual looking stone nestled in the ravine. It was about two feet by two feet in diameter and looked out of place. Somewhat flat, it resembled what one could imagine as the ocean floor: smooth ridges, a few shallow holes in the middle, and deeper trenches along the outside edges. I asked the Lord what it was about this rock that compelled me to stop and take notice. "This is your life," was His reply. I pondered that a moment while studying the characteristics of the rock at my feet. I realized that I too had holes in my life, ups and downs, and deep trenches carved around the edges. The small area where moss and algae had grown and hardened reminded me of scars and surface wounds. The thorns in my life appeared in the form of a section of cactus that had broken off and landed between a couple of the ridges. And then the Holy Spirit said to me, "Your life is in the palm of My hand." Tears. I was astonished to recognize the remarkable resemblance of the rock to a cupped hand. More tears as I contemplated Isaiah 49:16. *What an awesome God!* He has such a beautiful way of illustrating His promises and making them real.

## OBEY

God doesn't need to be understood, just heard. So many times I experienced an urge or prompting from the Holy Spirit to do something but with no explanation of why. For example, one morning I set out for my walk and felt I should walk in a different direction. Going opposite of the way I would normally go, I walked through a neighborhood and admired the flowers and gardens growing in the yards. Winding up one street and down another, I ended up by the high school where a couple of boys were scaling a twelve-foot-high chain-link fence. *Yikes!* I prayed a quick prayer for their safety and continued my jaunt through town and back home. Later, I recalled my walk and wondered, *What if God had intentionally had me walk that way knowing I would see the boys and pray for them? What if I hadn't been there or prayed? Who knows?*

The first day of school back at my old job—the one I didn't want—I arrived about twenty minutes early. Not ready to go inside yet, I felt I needed to walk around the school building and the property to pray. I really didn't know what to pray for, so I prayed in the Spirit (Romans 8:26).

On multiple other occasions I was led to make the loop around the school in the same manner. During PE class, I prayed while walking the track behind the school with the kids (actually they ran, I walked). I began to pray that the school would someday become known as the school of Jesus Christ. Not that it would necessarily be a private Christian school but that the teachers, staff, and students would know the Lord. There was already a good number of believers working and attending the school, and I prayed for more.

As an aide, one of my duties was to man the crosswalk in the mornings when children were dropped off. I loved greeting all the kiddos and their parents and intentionally tried to pray for each one every day, mostly in the Spirit as I didn't know what was going on in all of their lives. I did that for two years. On my very last day, I felt it necessary to make one last circle around the school. I had no idea that about a year later a new church would be having services and children's Bible studies in the gymnasium every Sunday. *What an awesome God.*

Then there was the time God planted a thought in my heart to attend the annual Blossom Festival to hand out money. It's a big celebration held in the spring at a local park. Vendors of all kinds sell their wares. There are food booths galore and entertainment for young and old alike. People come from all around to attend the spring festivities. I pictured myself handing out quarters to the kids, but wow! That would be a lot of kids and a lot of quarters. However, that was not God's plan.

A month or so before the event, certain dollar amounts, and certain Scriptures stood out to me, and I made note of both. Then I started seeing visions of particular people who I did not know. Five people, to be exact: two of whom I had a pretty clear picture of, the other three not so much. As the date approached, God started to match the Scripture and dollar amounts to the people He showed me. Some were to receive quite a bit more than others. To help myself not look so conspicuous, I put the money inside a card in which I wrote the specific Bible verse given to me. In the bottom right-hand corner of the envelope, I drew a symbol that would give me a clue to whom that envelope belonged. On one I drew a stick figure for a reserved looking teenage boy or girl. A hat on another for the lady with dark brown hair wearing a straw hat and red scarf tied loosely around her neck. And a B for the big burly biker dude with tattoo-covered biceps, a scruffy beard, wearing a black leather vest with chains. *Oh my.* The other two I left blank except for the words: The Lord Wants to Bless You Today.

The closer to the day of the festival, the more nervous I got and wondered what in the world I was doing. This was a crazy idea, and it is so not me to go hunt people down in a crowd and give them a card containing money. What would I say to them? How would I know where they were? What if I give the envelope to the wrong person? Why am I doing this in the first place? What if I copped out? What if these people did not get to read the Scripture that was meant for them that day? What if the person whose pocketbook was empty and had a bill that needed to be paid didn't get the money? What if they just needed a surprise to make their day or to bring a smile to their face, and it didn't come? Someone would miss a blessing from God that they may not have known they needed, and I didn't want to be the one who kept that from happening. *O Lord, is this really of You?* I knew it was and I had to obey, but boy oh boy, was this a big step out of my comfort zone!

The day arrived and Laurae, Syris, and I headed to the parade first. I needed encouragement and help to spot the individuals. Bumping elbows with the people on the crowded streets, I saw a young couple with a newborn baby. *How sweet,* I thought as I passed them by. A few steps later I sensed one of the unmarked envelopes belonged to them. Turning around, I approached them and commented on the infant, handing them the envelope. "God wants to bless you today,"

I said, and they graciously accepted. *Whew! That wasn't so bad. One down and four to go.*

I prayed as I walked through the mobs of people perusing all the goodies. *Lord, show me who is next.* It wasn't long before I saw a teen walking alongside her grandfather, I presumed. She was tall and thin and walked with her eyes downward. She smiled at something her grandpa said but didn't look up. I felt strongly to give her the stick figure envelope.

It was close to noon and the temperature was rising. I meandered through the park several times and realized there must've been a motorcycle rally going on that weekend. There were big burly biker dudes everywhere. I really did not look forward to approaching one of them. *Ugh.* Strolling past a vendor's booth, I noticed a woman standing behind the table in the shade of her tent. She had dark brown hair and wore a straw hat and had a red scarf around her neck. *That can't be her. She has a booth.* Why I thought that mattered, I don't know. I said hello, she nodded, and I moved on. I continued my search. Not having any luck and coming full circle, I came upon the lady in the booth again. She fit the description and I hadn't seen anyone else who did, so I took a chance and walked up to her. She was now alone. She looked hot, tired, and somewhat unhappy. I told her I believed God wanted to bless her today and handed her the envelope. She rolled her eyes and took the card.

Sipping a fresh lemonade, I sat at a picnic table in the food court area. Bikers were everywhere, most of them with beards, tattoos, and black vests. I really didn't want to do this and thought maybe I should wait and come again tomorrow. Laurae and Syris had left a long time ago, so my moral support was gone. I prayed. And I prayed some more. Just as I was contemplating leaving for the day, I saw him. My heart pounded from nervousness. The Holy Spirit confirmed he was the one. Arms the size of telephone poles and colorfully decorated with tattoos of all shapes and sizes, he wore a black leather vest and chains and his unruly hair was escaping the confines of his do-rag. He was accompanied by a woman also clad in motorcycle apparel and a young girl about ten years old. Hands shaking, I forced myself to take a step in his direction. The woman and young girl entered a booth, and Goliath stood alone eating his burger. This was my chance. *Holly, get a grip*. Looking up, I said, "Excuse me, I have a gift from the Lord for you." He looked at me with surprisingly gentle eyes and a slight smile "What did you say?" he asked. *Oh dear*, I thought, *I have to repeat myself*. His voice struck me funny, and I almost laughed. I was expecting rough and gruff but instead it was a much higher pitch than I was prepared for. Again, I said, "Here is a gift from the Lord." "From whom?" he asked. "From the Lord," I repeated. "Oh, well, tell him I said thank you," he offered.

He smiled, I smiled and then I turned and booked it out of the crowd to the parking lot and never looked back. That was enough for one day. I had one more envelope, but it would have to wait. And that it did. I ended up giving it to a Sonic worker at the drive-up window several weeks later. I had to trust that assignment was a blessing to the recipients. It was definitely a test of my faith and a boost in courage and boldness. I was going to need it.

*Jedd and Laurae after her high school graduation.*

*One of many bridges we carefully crossed to reach a village.*

*A long march through the mud was an glorious adventure.*

*Kids enjoying a PNG style 'jungle' gym.*

*The YWAM PNG medical ship.*

*Oro Province welcome*

*I looked forward to my daily 'wash wash' in the Kumusi River.*

*Praying for the homebound was the highlight of my days in the villages.*

*The local villagers cut notches in a log for easier access to the falcon in low tide.*

# 16

## LAND OF THE UNEXPECTED

Was I really doing this? Traveling to the other side of the world, alone, to study health care for the sick in developing countries with people I have never met, most of whom were half my age, for six months? Not a typical introvert's dream.

The fragrance of plumeria greeted me in Australia, as it had in Kona. Fringe-a-penny (the common name for plumeria) and towering palm trees replaced the pines and cottonwoods of Colorado. The ocean and nearby Great Barrier Reef were a nice and welcomed contrast to snowcapped mountains, as was the hot humid weather. I could definitely get used to the climate. I'm not one for frigid temperatures.

YWAM Townsville, in North Queensland, was conveniently located within walking distance to stores, The Strand (a favorite local hangout along the beach with walking/jogging trails), and the infamous Castle Hill (a three hundred sixty-degree overlook of the Townsville area, ocean, and Magnetic Island). The 1,483 man-made steps (many of which were higher and deeper than the average stair height) and natural rock made the climb up Castle Hill all the more difficult.

## HOT TOPICS

I shared a room with three roommates young enough to be my daughters. There I learned to discipline myself to study ten to twelve hours a week to complete my homework and try my best to learn this new foreign language. The medical lingo and terms were difficult enough but when pronounced with an Australian accent it made it much harder. It had been thirty-five years since I had been a student, and not a very dedicated one at that. Since God had called me into this, I chose to get the most out of this training as possible, challenging as it was.

Anatomy and physiology classes were my initiation into the medical field, and it wasn't for dummies. My brain was stretched from the very beginning. Tropical disease and diagnosis, malnutrition, sanitation and water-borne illnesses, tuberculosis, skin disease and infections, snake and insect bites—we covered them all. We learned mother and child wellness with hands-on practice sessions, learned how to give subcutaneous, intramuscular, and intradermal vaccinations with a saline solution. First the needles penetrated an orange, then we stabbed each other. Who would've known all those injections I gave Jedd were a prerequisite for the upcoming outreaches? Overall, what interested me the most was the section on parasites and worms.

LAND OF THE UNEXPECTED

Ear, nose, and throat study was my least favorite. Ear wax made me gag—*the* worst! I'd rather clean up vomit.

## KANGAROOS, CROCS, AND SPIDERS, OH MY!

I loved the fact that our IPHC leader loved the outdoors and scheduled hiking excursions on the weekends. For the trekking team, of which I was a part, it was mandatory. She led us on some amazing four- to nine-mile hikes in the Aussie wilderness. What better way to see the country than on foot? I had to stop often and thank God for blessing me and urging me months earlier to get in shape. I would not have wanted to miss any of this.

It was on one of those adventures that I saw the biggest spider in my entire life. It was as big as my hand and the web stretched between two large trees over the trail. It was fascinating, colorful, and creepy.

Castle Hill was another training ground. The qualifying hike to the top with a thirty-pound pack in less than forty-five minutes was the ultimate test for the trekkers. I held my own with my young teammates and made it in thirty-one minutes. Way to go grandma!

Occasionally we saw a wallaby on someone's lawn. To me, the foreigner, it was an amazing sight, and I couldn't get enough of the local wildlife and colorful birds. Just as visitors to Colorado sometimes are amazed at seeing deer roaming the streets or grazing in a yard, undeterred by human spectators.

At Billabong Wildlife Sanctuary we had the opportunity to see animals up close and personal. I hugged a kangaroo, petted a wombat and koala bear, draped a five-foot python over my shoulders, and held a small crocodile. That had never been on my bucket list either but hey, might as well. Eating green ants on Maggie Island was another experience I had to try. Honestly, they weren't bad.

## "ORO ORO ORO"

Papua New Guinea (PNG) is known as the Land of the Unexpected. That couldn't have been more true than when we landed in Port Moresby, and I heard myself say out loud, "This feels like home." Now that was unexpected.

**Oh, my goodness, this country, the little bit that I've seen is beautiful. I'm really pretty excited about this journey God is taking me on. Pretty nervous too. Tears came to my eyes when we arrived, the atmosphere just feels like home. Yikes!**

Flip charts in hand, we paired up and took to the streets of Alotau to look for willing individuals to share simple health care awareness. It was our first assignment before we jumped into doing clinics. Large crowds of people walked barefoot to and from the outdoor produce and fish markets that lined the beetle nut–stained streets. No one turned us down as we shared the basics of nutrition, personal hygiene, malaria prevention, and well-baby care. Oral hygiene was another important area of concern as many people, children included, chew *bui* (beetle nut) dipped in powdered lime (not the citrus kind). The combination produces a red juice which is spit out like chewing tobacco. *Bui*'s addictive effects are similar to cigarettes, and it can cause cancer of the mouth. We also had the opportunity to offer prayer to anyone we made contact with. Now this was something I truly enjoyed: teaching and praying.

Our initial accommodation on the mission field was the Alotau sports stadium. For a week we camped out on the concrete under the bleachers, packed together like sardines under our *mozzy* (mosquito) nets. Our next stop we slept a few nights on empty hospital beds in a vacant room at Kokoda Hospital. My favorite accommodation was in Pija, our home base for about three weeks. There we had a small "guest house" in the middle of nowhere next to the Kumusi River. The so-called house consisted of an open-air, three-room hut on stilts. Each room was separated by a palm lattice divider and a colorful *lap-lap* (wraparound skirt) as a door. I shared a room with two other girls. There was just barely enough space for our sleeping bags and backpacks to fit under our individual mozzy nets. The sound of the jungle at night was as refreshing as the moist warm air that penetrated the walls. I absolutely loved it. Surrounded by lush tropical plants, shrubs and trees, I thought there couldn't be a more beautiful place. I hadn't seen nothin' yet.

At Pija, the pit toilet, which was a fifteen-yard walk behind the house, consisted of a hole with a tarp tied up around it for privacy. The middle of the slow-moving river served as our bathtub (wash wash), our never-ending faucet for drinking water (that we pumped through a filter), our laundry machine, and our dish washer. *Never in a million years.*

Sometime during this trip, I remembered that shortly after my husband and I had gotten married, he said he wanted to take a guided trip down the Amazon river and to camp in the jungles—for fun.

At the time, I thought that was a ridiculously stupid idea: *Are you kidding?! Sitting in a boat under a scorching sun; floating in unknown territory with snakes, spiders, bugs, and unknown creatures lurking in the muddy waters; and camping in the jungle?* That was not even remotely close to my kind of enjoyment. And yet, here I was, in Papua New Guinea doing just that—and loving it. With God we can expect the unexpected, and, if needed, He will change our heart and make known His will and His plans and purposes to us (Ephesians 1:8-9).

"*Oro oro oro. Oro kaiva.*" The customary Oro Province welcome rang out as we entered the villages to set up clinics for the day. I learned to introduce myself in Pigin (the somewhat universal language of PNG, although there are over seven hundred tribal languages nationwide), and to ask a few important clinic questions. After a while I understood a lot more than I could speak.

I was impressed by and respected the leadership qualities of our fearless team leader. Not yet thirty years old, she demonstrated the maturity of someone way beyond her years in experience and authority. She was an adventurist, very mindful and considerate of others. She had discernment and sought the Lord. I liked how she was not just the leader, the facilitator, organizer of logistics, but also a member and servant on the team. We were in good hands, plus it was helpful that she could fluently speak the language.

Large groups of mamas with a baby or two on the hips gathered around the village center waiting to vaccinate their children. Never ever did I imagine myself filling syringes in the middle of a jungle and poking needles into precious little dark-skinned, curly black-haired children. (The vision I had as I stood before the altar years earlier had become reality. Not in Africa as I had thought but in the remote areas of Papua New Guinea.) We white "ghosts" (*dim dims*) were scary enough to the little ones—many of whom had never seen a white person before—let alone been stabbed with a needle by them, and not just once but several times.

Those with fever, cough, diarrhea, and vomiting or with severe burns and injuries waited patiently to be seen in the See and Treat hut, our makeshift open-air doctor's office. I was uncomfortable prescribing a course of treatment even though I was confident of the diagnosis. I was grateful we had local doctors with whom to confer and confirm each case. Anyone with ear issues I discreetly handed over to another team member for fear of gagging and puking.

So what does my fearless leader do? She calls me away from the malaria testing table where dozens of rapid tests were lined up waiting for a verification of a positive or negative outcome, and she leads me into a closed room to incise a large boil on a child's leg and drain out the infection. Of course, he was given an injection to deaden the area first. Skin is much tougher than I had imagined, even when you have a razor blade. It's even harder trying to pierce it with a needle and thread to suture an open wound. Yes, she had me stitch up a young woman's wound too. I really didn't have time to refuse, but I did give her a "you've got to be kidding me" look as she handed me the large, curved needle. She walked me through the process, and I tried not to let the patient know I had never done stitches before, nor had I even practiced on a leather handbag, which would have been quite helpful.

Student after student entered the meagerly supplied classroom and lay face up on the teacher's desk where we performed a simple routine spleen check. A sweet young girl with unkempt hair shyly lifted her oversized, torn, and dirt-stained shirt as she lay down. I was surprised to see a two-inch diameter open wound on her chest. It resembled a burn that left the skin raw and wet looking. Through an interpreter I learned the youngster had been climbing a tree and unknowingly hugged a *shongololo* (a millipede). In self-defense the large multi-legged critter flipped over and secreted a fluid containing hydrochloric acid onto the girl's flesh, which ate away several layers. No wonder our local guide had urged me to move along quickly as I stooped over as far as I could to get a close-up photo of the nice black specimen that was crossing the trail. I had no idea they were armed and dangerous. I once asked one of the locals which spiders I should watch out for, and he quickly replied, "All of them." Now I could add *shongololos* to my list of spiders and snakes and other unsafe jungle critters. Some of the world's most deadly snakes live in PNG and Australia. And to think I was sleeping outside with only a mozzy net for protection (and God, of course).

Speaking of the creepy crawlers, there was one that stood guard over the pit toilet while we stayed in Agenehambo. Whether it was the enormous amount of water I drank during the day or the effects of getting a bit older, occasionally I needed to make a trip to the toilet in the middle of the night. This was a very unfortunate problem for my roommates as we were not to go out at night alone. I needed a potty partner, if you will. I wore a small head lamp so I could see and keep my hands free. I was intrigued by a large bulbous, velvety gray spider that appeared to be the night watchman night after night in the corner. He was not disturbed by my presence, so I figured if I let him be, he would not bother me. As my light shone on him, two brilliant green eyes like emeralds set in a fine piece of jewelry stared back at me.. God's creation was on display in a dark corner of our outdoor latrine.

One night my eight-legged friend was not visible, which made me a bit nervous not knowing where he was hiding. Later that day I saw him munching on a plump tropical cockroach. Made sense. The shallow pit was crawling with them.

Many nights I lay in my sleeping bag and asked God why He had called me into the medical mission field. I was loving the adventure, but I was not enjoying the clinic stuff. *"If this is truly what You want me to do,"* I prayed, *"please change my heart."* I had to trust Him in this journey.

## WHEN THE VOLCANO BLOWS, STAY PUT

On rare occasions I was blessed to make a home visit to pray with the elderly, hold a hand, and listen to stories. I preferred that to needles and crying babies any day.

Barevoturu is a gorgeous mountain village. There, eighty-six-year-old John Lyle shared a story from his younger years. He grew up in this village and was elected the village chief or counselor for many years. In the 1950s or 60s the volcano that rose above the place they had settled and called home began to rumble. Many villagers fled in fear as smoke, ash, and fire came down the mountain. The people living in upper Barevoturu decided to stay and trust God. They constructed a white line on the ground, presumably with sand or shells, from one side of the village to the other. They placed a Bible on the line and gathered in prayer. They watched as the billows of smoke, fire, and ash closed in on them. Just when they thought their efforts were in vain, they stood awestruck as the heavy dark clouds stopped at the white line and receded. The village was spared by the grace of God, and from that day on all the people believed and were saved. Some might say that is impossible, but nothing is impossible with God (Luke 1:37; Jeremiah 32:17).

Shortly after we heard the inspiring and powerful account of the miraculous act of God, we were blessed with a hike through the jungle on the path that wound up that very mountain to a memorial. Our local guide walked ahead swinging his machete back and forth to clear the vines and vegetation that had begun to take over the narrow trail. I think he also scouted the area for unwelcome long slithering reptiles. Just a hunch.

Half-naked children scampered barefoot alongside us in the undergrowth as we *dim dims* carefully navigated our next steps. Being Sunday, I wore a flowing black cotton skirt and my comfy but well-worn Crocs—not the best for hiking. The thirty-minute hike up to the memorial was absolutely beautiful. I was still in awe of my surroundings. Was I really in the jungles of PNG or was it a dream? I pictured myself in the *Jungle Book* story. Children were playing, climbing trees, and swinging from the rope-like vines hanging from the branches. *Incredible!*

Quite suddenly, the clouds rolled in. The locals knew the signs in the sky and urgently persuaded us to turn back. But not soon enough. The rain came down mightily and almost immediately the trails became streams of water. I'm sure it was a comical sight. A white-skinned gray-haired *bubu* (grandma) dressed in her Sunday best, slipping and sliding in the mud, trying to stay upright, all the while her clothes became drenched. With one hand I attempted to pull up the hem of my skirt under the weight of the water and the other stretched out to keep balance on the uneven terrain. Eventually several attentive youths saw my predicament and came to my rescue. One carried my day pack while another took my hand as we surfed the trail. I was laughing and loving every minute of it. I had not experienced that kind of joy in months, if not years. Jedd would surely have loved the adventure.

## BANANAS

There is nothing like a freshly picked banana. Several days had passed since I had eaten one, and I really hoped the village we were going to that day would offer us a large bunch of the yellow fruit. Upon arrival I selfishly scanned the area—not a banana tree in sight. Oh well, I would survive. My daily ration of Emnaus (hard chicken-flavored biscuits) and canned tuna with red chili would have to suffice. Actually, it was quite good, and I never tired of it.

As I recall, we had a particularly slow start that day as we waited for the locals to *wash wash* and others to walk in from nearby villages with their children. In the distance I recognized a woman with whom I had shared a bit of my story in a previous village. She kind of took a liking to me as I reminded her of a bubu from England who ministered to her years before. When she heard our team was visiting Hajeka, she and her daughter made a three-and-a-half-hour trek from their Puremo village home that morning, hoping to see me. She brought me a pamphlet on grief (no idea where she acquired something like that), a traditional handmade *bilim* (a handbag), and a huge bunch of bananas. Really! I cried. Silly I know, but it's the truth. God blessed me with bananas and used a woman and her daughter to bring them to me. I thanked them before they made the long trek home to spend the rest of the day working in the gardens.

## WHEN YOU GOTTA GO, YA GOTTA GO

Mid-June 2016, we loaded all of our gear into our backpacks and trekked to Ariho, a village in the swampland. We had the traditional Oro welcome as we passed through the village, escorted by a couple men in native dress and carrying flower-decorated palms. In the village center, Pastor Joseph opened with a word of prayer, and I immediately felt a part of the community. The pastor moved out of his four-room hut to make room for us for the four to five days of our visit. We gratefully took up residence in his modest home.

I guess being older has some advantages as I was given the pastor's small room, complete with a two-inch mattress to sleep on. Luxury! A small corner shelf was just big enough for my Bible and sixteen-ounce coffee cup with space for my pack underneath. An open window with no screen overlooked the courtyard and village center—a room with a view. The seven-rung lean-to ladder was our access to the inside of the hut, which stood about seven feet off the ground.

Most of the homes in PNG are on stilts for several reasons. One, it provides extra air flow in the hot humid climate. Second, it keeps the huts dry in times of heavy rains or high tide in areas where the tide raises the rivers and blankets the land each day. Lastly, many huts have their cooking quarters located underneath which allows the smoke from the cooking fires to rise and repel the Anopheles mosquitos that carry malaria. Not all families have access to mozzy nets, and some would rather use them as fishing nets and risk the chances of getting bitten.

The pastor not only gave up his home for us but had instructed a few tribesmen to build two somewhat enclosed bucket shower areas and also to dig a new pit toilet. We had to carry in our own supply of toilet paper unless we wanted to use grass or leaves, or go without.

I did not sleep well the first night. There was so much noise. People were singing and playing guitar, frogs croaked, people were working under the hut and elsewhere, critters were crawling around in and on the house, plus I had to pee. Go figure. I didn't want to wake my nighttime pee partner, so I held it until the sun came up. By then people were building cooking fires, chopping wood, sweeping the grounds, worshipping, and the dogs! The dogs yipped, yelped and barked all the time.

As our outreach in the bush came to an end, the long hot days in the villages doing clinics caught up with me. I was twenty-five years older than most of my teammates, not that that should be an excuse, but I was getting tired. So tired. I hadn't been sleeping well. Noise, and having to pee in the middle of the night had been the major issues . One night I had to go so badly I tried to wake my partner and my team leader but neither woke up. *What to do?* It was nowhere near time to get up, and I knew I couldn't wait for the sun to rise. I considered taking the chance of going down the ladder in the dark and walking to the pit alone but thought better of it. There was a reason we were asked to have a partner, and I didn't want to break the safety rules. I thought about squatting in the corner of the room over a hole in the floor, but what if someone was sleeping directly below? I also did not want to get any cooking pots wet. I was desperate, extremely uncomfortable to the point of feeling a bit nauseous. Once again, I tried waking the girls with no luck. I could not reach far enough under the mozzy net to nudge them, and I didn't want to yell and wake up the others. Obviously, they had no trouble sleeping. The predicament was real! I was running out of ideas and options. *Hmm, I do have my large coffee mug and my water bottle.* The water bottle opening was too small to try to figure out in the dark so the coffee cup it was. What a relief!

Come morning, I had another problem. The coffee cup was literally full to the brim. It would've been impossible to carry it outside and down the ladder. Plus, the village was abuzz with morning duties. *Good grief.* Carefully, I emptied it into my water bottle. A little less conspicuous, bringing a full water bottle to the pit toilet. I don't think anyone noticed that I didn't bring it back out again. The water bottle was no loss really, it had melted into a C shape when I attempted to pour boiling water in it to sanitize it earlier in the outreach. If anyone was so inclined to peer down the hole, they would have seen a purple water bottle glistening in the morning sun.

## SHIP CALLING

For several months I had this tugging desire to pursue a return trip in autumn to volunteer on the ship that delivers health care to some of the most remote areas in the nation. I really wasn't interested in doing clinics, and I let God know it . . . often. He would have to change my heart if that was what my future held. I spent more time wondering and complaining and less time thanking God for the amazing opportunities to serve His people in what I could only describe as the most beautiful place I had ever seen. Why was I constantly trying to figure out the who, what, where, when, how, and why? Relying on my own thoughts instead of seeking God's perspective was getting me nowhere. The more I leaned on my own understanding, the less I knew. It is no wonder God impressed 1 Thessalonians 5:16-17 strongly upon my heart: *Rejoice always. Pray without ceasing. Be thankful in all circumstances as that is the will of God for my life.*

My experiences on the few boats I had been on in my life had not been pleasant. I got seasick. I would much rather keep my feet on dry land. As I prayed, I was led to read portions of the book of Acts. Certain words and phrases popped up as I read chapter 20, which persuaded me to pray harder.

**Help the weak. It is more blessed to give than to receive. House to house. I do not account my life of any value nor as precious to myself. To the ship. Rise and go . . . and there you will be told all that is appointed for you to do.**

Three days later I filled out the application for outreaches number seven and eight in October and November. In no time at all my request was reviewed, and I was recommended to be a community engagement leader. *Me? A leader? Good grief.*

Two weeks later I landed in Texas for a short stay with Laurae and family (they had recently moved to the Dallas area) before I headed back to Colorado. It was so good to see them. I missed them terribly. Little Esther was already nine months old.

Again, I experienced the reverse culture shock. Reality set in that I was no longer in the bush where life was hard but simple. Instead, I was back in the modern complex chaos of conveniences, materialism, flashy lights, worldly lusts and desires. *Ugh*.

While in the Lone Star State I received an email from the YWAM ships. Would I consider staying on for outreach nine as well to keep consistency in the leadership? Wow, approximately nine weeks on a ship. I had just about that same amount of time to come up with the money to fund my next mission.

# 17

## IN OVER MY HEAD

God never ceases to amaze me. He delivered me from a reckless state of desperation and, through an innocent invitation from a nine-year old sweetheart on a playground, He saved me from eternal destruction where there is "weeping and gnashing of teeth" (Matthew 13:42; Luke 13:28); He gave me a peace, a strength, a joy, and a hope that defies all natural reason as He walked me through Jedd's death (Philippians 4:6-7); He blessed me with the miracle of life through a teenage pregnancy (Psalm 139:14); He guarded both my daughter and my husband from potentially fatal car accidents (Psalm 18:2); He graciously and faithfully answered my prayers of "whatever it takes" to bring my children into a saving grace relationship with Him (Mark 11:24); He restored all that was lost to Laurae and Syris after He rescued them from the fiery furnace of abuse (Jeremiah 29:11; 1 Peter 5:10); by His stripes I am healed of all cancer, sickness, and disease now and forever (Isaiah 53:5); He held my hand as I waited and agonized over a failing marriage with no reconciliation in sight and He released me at just the right time (Psalm 73:23-24); and He has honored my obedience to missions by decorating my journey with trips to Hawaii, Israel, India, Africa, Australia, and Papua New Guinea. How great is our God!

## HERE AM I, SEND ME

The Spirit of the Lord God is upon me, because the Lord has anointed me to bring good news to the poor, He has sent me to bind up the brokenhearted, to proclaim liberty to the captives, and the opening of the prison to those who are bound, to proclaim the year of the Lord's favor, and the day of vengeance of our God; to comfort all who mourn. (Isaiah 61:1-2)

God had told me that the skills I learned in IPHC were my ticket to get me into the places He wanted to take me. "Continue to follow Me," He said. "And I will show you things you could never imagine and what most people will never see." He was about to faithfully fulfill that promise as I prepared for my return as a volunteer on the ship.

I was blown away by the number of people who contacted me wondering how and where they could donate. It seemed totally backwards. Wasn't I the one who was supposed to be soliciting and making contacts? Even a gentleman I met on the plane contacted me and followed through with a generous donation.

An email from YWAM Townsville stated that my ship fees for three outreaches as a staff member totaled one thousand one hundred fifty dollars. And wouldn't you know it? I had one thousand one hundred forty nine left over in my IPHC account. *Is that not incredibly God or what?* I still had to come up with funds for my Visa, airfare, anti-malarial medications, travel insurance, and a little backup cash for unexpected expenses. I truly believe that when God asks you to do something, He will equip you and provide all your needs. He proved that to be true in my past, and I trusted He would do it again.

In the back of my mind a recurring thought kept surfacing: *Do not purchase a round-trip ticket. Do not purchase a round-trip ticket.* That concerned me a little. Was I supposed to stay longer than the three outreaches I originally committed to? *Yikes!* (Yes. By the end of the second outreach, I knew that God wanted me to commit to another three after the Christmas holiday. And wouldn't you know, before that commitment was up, I sensed the strong urge to put in for the last three outreaches before the ship returned to Townsville for refit. Oh my!)

My mom's memory seemed remarkably worse from when I left the first time, and I worried about her safety and well-being. I knew at some point a decision would have to be made, but right then she refused to see a doctor for any kind of evaluation. She often joked about having to live with one of her children someday so we could take care of her. "Who will take care of me if you leave? Who will feed me?" Laughing about it on the outside and crying and fearful on the inside. Guilt and more guilt.

I pondered, sobbed, and prayed about whether or not I should go ahead and return to PNG. I had to choose to trust God and believe

He had divine plans for me despite how I was feeling. Guilt is from the enemy, and I could not allow him to sway my decision. Matthew 10:37 says, "Whoever loves father or mother more than Me is not worthy of Me." The love of God and His will must take precedence over every other human relationship. It was hard!

On October 11, 2016, I held my mom close. With tears welling up, I released her into God's loving hands believing that He would care for her as I prepared to board my first leg of flights back to the Land of the Unexpected.

Here I was, embarking on another adventure to a tiny spot on the globe where one in five children die before the age of five. Where tuberculosis has become an epidemic, and where I would guess eighty percent of the population has no access to clean water or health, vision, or dental care, let alone an education. *Who am I that God would call me to such a remote area of the world, live on a medical ship, and lead teams of volunteers into places I've never been?*

## OH, THE PLACES I WILL GO

A small cabin with two twin beds about two feet apart, a couple cabinets, and a bathroom where you could pee, take a shower, and brush your teeth all at the same time would be my dwelling place for nine months. I couldn't believe I would live and work from a big white ship, a big white ship incredibly similar to the one I saw during a time of worship in Kona, Hawaii, during my DTS. A coincidence? I think not.

The YWAM PNG serviced five provinces. Some locations took us out into open water to miniature islands surrounded by pristine, crystal-clear waters in the outer edges of the Great Barrier Reef. Brilliant hues of red, orange, yellow, green, and blue corals decorated the ocean floor where colorful fish darted in and out of the underwater garden of eden. Curious pods of dolphins jumped and swam alongside the smaller boats as we jetted through their territory. The prehistoric-looking Rhinoceros beetles somehow made it onto the decks of the ship and were frequent visitors. Other times we ferried into shore in the twelve-passenger Falcon boats or the six-man Zodiacs to white sandy beaches lined with huts on stilts. Smoke from cooking fires dotted the hillsides behind the villages.

In Gulf and Western Provinces, we anchored away from shore and traveled by smaller boats up the muddy, crocodile-infested rivers deep into the jungles to some of the most remote villages in the world. I heard it said that if Western Province were a nation of its own, it would be considered the poorest in the world. It amazes me that just because the land looks lush and fruitful does not mean it is. PNG is absolutely beautiful, clearly paradise on earth. Yet its people struggle under harsh conditions: poor water, lack of variety of foods, difficult living conditions, and isolation. From the outside it is quite deceiving.

Western and Gulf are known for the rising and receding tides that leave the villages in deep standing water in high tide and in several feet of glorious mud in low tide. Many times we carefully made our way through the obstacle course of slick notched logs that served as ladders up the steep, miry banks and sketchy bridges and ladders that led into the rest huts or meeting areas in the village center. This infrastructure was familiar to the inhabitants but felt hazardous to us non-locals, who aren't normally barefoot. Being the older and partially gray-haired lady on the team had some advantages here. Rarely did I have to go it alone. If it wasn't a mama or two or a strong young man lending an arm, it was the children who came to my rescue.

Like most natives living in the more remote area of PNG, the people of Western and Gulf Province subsisted on farming, fishing, and the beetle nut. They are extremely hard workers. Even the children and *bubus* have handshakes that could crush a finger or two. Schools and aid posts are few and far between, as are markets carrying basic items. For some it might mean a half day walk for education or up to a two-day journey by dugout canoe for medical help and supplies. Working in the gardens or fishing kept many children from attending school on a regular basis. Teachers and health care workers often find the living conditions too extreme and difficult and therefore they do not stay long. Electricity, running water, and Digicel service (the local Internet provider) are pretty much nonexistent in most places. Some villages have been blessed with rain tanks for collecting rainwater, but if the tanks are not covered, they become breeding grounds for mosquitos. Malaria is an ongoing health issue and hard to resolve in the wet tropical climate. In the majority of the places we went, it was obvious their clothes were seconds from America and Europe. They were torn; full of holes; stained with mud, blood, sweat, and tears; and worn until the threads barely held together.

Once I chatted with a volunteer schoolteacher who shared in a cheerful voice, "We may be poor here on earth, but we will be rich in heaven." I loved his positive attitude and vision of eternal hope (James 2:5). That daily faith for provision, health, and hope despite what is seen and experienced in the natural world.

Sorcery and witchcraft are not uncommon practices in PNG, and several times I witnessed the effects of the power of darkness upon certain individuals. The demonic realm is real but thank God "for he who is in you is greater than he who is in the world" (1 John 4:4).

## LEADER?!

I spent the first few days on board the ship in meetings to learn the ropes of the new role I accepted: community engagement leader. Out of my comfort zone, overwhelmed, and feeling a bit in over my head (actually, that literally would come later on a harrowing boat ride), I pushed forward in my God-given assignment. My mentor and "yell for help" person was very encouraging and thorough as he explained my responsibilities on and off ship. I shadowed him for two days and then wham! I was on my own.

Our main goal in each village was to educate and bring health awareness to as many people as possible, be it in the schools where we talked to large groups of children or in the village center where we instructed the adults and mamas as they waited to be seen in the outdoor clinics. Simple cartoon style flip charts for malaria, tuberculosis, HIV/AIDS, nutrition, well-baby care, and personal hygiene made teaching easier and were great visual aids for the students.

Tag games involving human sized mosquitos and our favorite activity, Head, Shoulders, Knees and Toes, brought the awareness to life. That song must've been a PNG favorite, as every village knew the lyrics and body motions. To change it up a bit, we started singing in ridiculously slow motion with exaggerated movements. With each repetition, we increased our speed until we were moving and singing as fast as humanly possible. It always ended in an eruption of laughter. The children (and adults) pointed at the goofy bubu making a fool of herself. So not me, and yet I could hardly wait to do it again. (Plus, I desperately needed and welcomed the exercise, despite the hot steamy climate.)

There was always the opportunity to share a gospel message, and many times it was expected and appreciated. At first, I was hesitant and lacked the confidence to bring the Word of God into my teachings, but eventually that became my number one focus, and I really looked forward to sharing.

A thorough village assessment at each location was essential for future YWAM groups bringing health care and resources to the villagers later. The assessments addressed water and sanitation issues, whether or not the villages had a school and teachers available (many were volunteer), churches, an aid-post with qualified health care workers, and other needs and concerns. In each village we distributed items such as toothbrushes and paste, soap, school supplies, clothes, and Days 4 Girls pack (kits containing washable feminine hygiene supplies). The items were not meant to be freebies, and we always encouraged a trade or exchange for them. The people were more than happy to accommodate our request with fresh produce and coconuts (my favorite!). In the less fortunate villages, we asked that they teach us a song or traditional dance for the swap.

When time allowed, we mingled with the locals, prayed for them, visited the homebound, and organized soccer games. The biggest challenge was trying to find enough people who spoke English well enough to translate for us and the clinic workers.

Once back on the ship, and after dinner, I still had a good hour of work to do recording village assessment information and statistics for the day. Even though I was considered the team leader I still shared in the nightly responsibility of washing the team's work clothes for the day. With only three washers and three dryers on board and approximately ninety volunteers with dirty clothes, you can imagine the race to get your team changed and showered and their dirty clothes in the bucket before the next team. (Woe to those who forgot or neglected to write their names on the tag of their YWAM shirt since the entire boat load of individuals had identical work clothes!) It was a sad day for the slower racers when at midnight or 5 a.m. the next morning they were still folding their teammates' clothes in preparation for the new day. I know—I experienced being the last finisher of the race on a couple occasions.

At the end of each two-week outreach, after the volunteers had grabbed their bags and headed to the airport, the team leaders inventoried and restocked all the supplies from large freight containers that were held in the port cities where we docked as we waited for the next group to arrive. There were summaries and more paperwork to fill out, and the ship had to be thoroughly cleaned in anticipation of the next influx of volunteers from all around the world. Each fortnight I was assigned a new group of community engagement helpers, anywhere from two to ten people ranging from toddlers to seventy-year-olds. I then gave an orientation and training for the upcoming outreach in the Land of the Unexpected.

# 18

## RUINED FOR THE ORDINARY

### END IS NEAR

A thin layer of weathered skin hung loosely from his old and tired bones. His eyes were glazed and drool gradually escaping the corner of his mouth dripped to the ground. A peeled bush pole at the entrance to his hut supported his fragile frame from tipping over. Although his lips moved in agony, all he could force out was a tiny squeak. The end was near, and he and I both knew it. My heart ached as I remembered those last few days with Jedd. I wanted to hold him in a close embrace, but all I could do was pray. In the words of Mother Teresa I wanted him "to die within sight of a loving face." What an honor to be that face. I hope I was.

### PAIN, FOR COMFORT

Fifteen or so women, some nursing infants, were sitting cross-legged in a circle with their eyes fixed on me as I stumbled through a teaching on a topic requested by the PNG Provincial Health Organization. Domestic violence was a growing problem, and it was a topic I was very much out of my comfort zone talking about. The women's gazes dropped to the floor, and if it hadn't been for all the ruckus outside you could've heard a pin drop. "Are there any questions?" I asked, secretly hoping there weren't because I was sure I didn't have any answers.

A young woman dressed in black, shoulders covered, hesitantly raised her hand. "Do you have any children?" Not the question I expected but one I could answer. (Earlier that morning, one of my volunteers came to me in tears prior to loading our gear on the boats. She told me of her dream the night before in which one of her children had died. It scared her and brought back the grief of losing her eight-year-old son in a car accident. She couldn't imagine going through the pain again.) This was one of those instances where God uses our pain and suffering to comfort others (2 Corinthians 1:4). Shooting up a silent "help me" prayer, I answered her question with my story of Jedd.

"Sorry, sorry, sorry." In their accent it sounded like "soo-ree."

The lady in black then asked my volunteer the same question. More soo-rees from the women and tears flowed all around the room. The precious lady who had asked the question was in mourning for the recent death of her four-year-old. *Oh my.* How the Lord brings three women from different parts of the world together to love, comfort, and pray for each other is a beautiful mystery.

## THE DESTITUTE

A father with two young boys in tow led us to the village church where we would share our health awareness teachings. We lugged our large portfolio full of flip charts and tubs of soap, toothbrushes, and toothpaste across several hewn logs spanning water-filled ditches and up the ten rungs of the primitive ladder into the empty sanctuary. The uneven floorboards bent under our weight while other decaying pieces left open spaces in the planking. A modest altar was the only thing that distinguished this hut from the others in the area. There were fewer than twenty people present to listen to our prepared talk. Midway through one teaching, I choked up and lost it. Tears streamed down my face, and I could not force myself to teach anymore.

Here we were, miles from anywhere, deep in the jungle where the only transportation is by boat or dugout canoe in crocodile-infested rivers. I understood the idea and how teaching was meant to be beneficial, but here it seemed absolutely pointless. Take prevention of malaria for example. Number one is to rid the area of Anopheles mosquito breeding grounds: standing water. What good is it to tell them that when the river tides leave them in knee-deep water for half of every day? Mosquito nets help but unfortunately many families use them as fishing nets. Nutrition, personal hygiene, giving birth in a hospital or aid post—all of these are most definitely important, but when a market or hospital is a full day's paddle, or more, away they make do with what they have. In my western mindset they were literally just surviving. Their life is so hard, and their needs are so great. I prayed a desperate prayer for God's mercy and hope to come down from heaven. I could not personally fathom the strength, perseverance, and endurance each person had to muster up every morning just to make it through another day, and yet this was life as they knew it and it had been for generations.

## LOVE IN ACTION

On a happier note, I was really touched one morning by a simple act of kindness. The Falcon was fully loaded with gear and a new set of volunteers. As we made our way up the river to yet another remote village, we spotted a very long dugout canoe barely wide enough to accommodate the width of your bottom side coming our way. In it were nine passengers, five of them children. We slowed way down so as to avoid flipping their already unstable mode of transport in the wake of our boat. A pair of volunteers, father and son, had brought some balls and wondered if they could give some to the children. The family in the canoe didn't appear fearful, but I'm sure they were quite curious why a motorboat full of strangers, obviously from countries other than their own, would approach them in their territory. You could see the whites of the eyes of the little ones as we drew closer. Very carefully we pulled up next to them, said hello, tossed a ball to each of the youngsters, and pulled away. Beaming faces smiling from ear to ear were just a reminder we can show the love of Jesus anywhere and anytime with just a smile and small gesture of giving. It was so random, but it touched me in a beautiful, unexpected way.

## BEYOND HOPE

"Would you please come pray for my mother?" asked a middle-aged man in the village of Pirupiru. "She has a growth on her stomach." The mother was not physically able to come to the clinic, and he looked seriously concerned. Not knowing for sure what I might encounter, I asked one of the volunteer doctors who knew the local language to accompany me.

We climbed up the ladder into the dark one-room hut, crawled in, and sat on the floor facing an elderly woman who greeted us with a quizzical smile. The son explained we had come to pray and give her medicine. Naked except for a *laplap*, she sat leaning against a support pole, unable to move. She was so extremely thin you could see the detail of every facial bone under her skin, and she breathed heavily and laboriously. The growth in her abdomen created a protrusion that left her looking like she was full term with triplets. The weight of the tumor was too much for her weak skeleton.

Her husband and two grown sons sat in the corner of the scanty home. A few bananas rested on the floor in the opposite corner, a couple mugs hung on the wall, and a small cooking fire smoldered in a large seashell in the middle of the hut, creating a cloud of smoke between us and the *bubu*. The doctor had to explain to her family that medicine would not be of any help except for pain, and the amount available was only enough for thirty days. Unfortunately, cancer treatment is rare in PNG, and a person would have to make their way to the larger port cities to receive a diagnosis and help. The woman was dying. We prayed.

If I had my choice of ministry, I would choose to do home visits all day. Visit the sick, elderly, disabled, crippled, dying, and destitute. If nothing else, I longed to pray, to hold their hand, and to tell them they are loved.

## MISSING TOES

The handsome fifteen-year-old boy was leaning against a tree with homemade crutches under his arms when we arrived at his hut. It was a five-minute walk through the bush from the village center. Open oozing infectious ulcers on his lower extremities had begun to migrate up his legs. He said he was not in pain, and the light in his eyes as he spoke almost made me believe he was being honest. He did not grimace as he stood talking with us. His father had told us in the clinic that his son's toes had been falling off. All the while I was thinking he meant his toenails, but upon observation, I noticed the young man was missing every toe on both feet. The doctor believed it was a case of leprosy or yaws and treated him the best that he could with what he had.

In the bush, when health care is not readily available, people must resort to home remedies, herbs, or see witch doctors in serious cases when nothing else seems to work. In the case of a severe headache, I was told that they believe if you make an incision in the forehead, the pressure will release, and the pain will drain out. *Oh my!*

God had told me that I would see things and places that most people will never see. Well, I had absolutely no idea the extent of it all. Besides the unsurpassed beauty of PNG, strange growths and diseases, there was an array of out of the ordinary sights and experiences yet to behold.

# 19

## | RESPITE |

Every time I turn around God is blessing me in one way or another. Since outreaches did not operate over the Christmas holiday, I returned to Townsville and stayed on the YWAM base for some welcome R and R. I had a studio apartment all to myself. I felt as if I was living in luxury. I had a private patio that overlooked the courtyard, a queen-sized bed, a huge bathroom (in comparison to the one on the ship), a kitchenette, and a flat-screen TV that I never turned on. What a treat!

While checking my online financial status, I noticed a few large deposits above and beyond what my monthly donors committed to. It was enough to cover all my fees for the next three outreaches plus my airfare back to PNG. Just another great example that God provides for all of our needs and even more than we could think or ask when we partner with Him in His plans and purposes (Ephesians 3:20).

Three and a half weeks of practically no specific duties or plans was truly satisfying and much needed. Long walks along the beach, fresh local produce, lounging with a good book and a cup of coffee, prayer without interruptions, and communicating with family and friends via Facebook were the highlights of my days.

Not everything with me was hunky-dory, though, at least not physically. While exercising on the ship one day, I twisted my knee. One day it would feel fine. The next it would be stiff and swollen. In addition, my fingers, ankles, feet, and neck decided to ache at random. Charlie horses in my calves and arches woke me at night, and I writhed in discomfort until I could work out the spasms. And just when I thought my digestive system was feeling normal again, I would suddenly experience the same nausea and urgency that came over me so many mornings on the ship. The athlete's foot fungus that I had acquired was now spreading to the tops of my feet and ankles. It was almost impossible to keep my feet dry long enough to get rid of it. Plus, ever since the muddy walks in Western Province, I had developed a striking orange "polish" on my toenails. It appeared to be unique to me as I didn't see anyone else sporting such colorful toes. But overall, I figured that if this was as bad as it was going to get, I was in pretty good shape.

That Townsville visit refreshed and invigorated me with a new excitement and courage to keep standing and move forward for what would be six more months of community engagement.

# 20

## ADVENTURES IN PARADISE

### ON THE POT

A ramshackle hut, the sketchiest up until that point, surrounded a black hole approximately six-foot square. Two or three narrow logs crisscrossed the hole in both directions. One would have to balance on the unstable logs and squat over the dark pit. It appeared to be a couple feet deep, but there was no telling for sure in the filtered light. The tarp that served as the door was so weathered you could almost see through it. I attempted to hold it up, but finally I figured if someone sees me, they see me. It was more important to latch on to a pole to keep from falling into the dank steaming mess below that was abuzz with flies. The logs I chose to step on were soft and bent under my weight. Thankfully, they didn't break, and I escaped unscathed with an empty bladder. Whew!

In each new village the first thing I did was find a mama who would be kind enough to show us visitors where the toilet was, if there was one. If there wasn't, they were more than happy to stand guard and shoo away any unwelcome visitors who might be in the vicinity. In one particular village, the accommodations happened to be a long-drop toilet built over a steep gully littered with rubbish, pointed sticks from dead bush plants, and whatever the rains washed in. Basically, it was a one-seater outhouse on stilts, hence the name long-drop toilet. There was no plumbing to hide what was dropping. Doing your business was everybody's business. To get to it, a person had to do a balancing act on the two-foot-wide split plank that stretched a good twelve feet to the outhouse. There were no handrails to guard against falling the eight feet into the rubbish. (It was a good thing I was no longer afraid of heights!) The mamas insisted it was safe, but I wasn't so confident. I suggested using the bush, but they assured me it was ok. *Yikes!* With one woman holding my left hand and another holding my right, I sidestepped my way to the small, enclosed toilet. The mamas were right, the bridge was sturdy enough. But I didn't trust my balance for the return trip, so I asked them to please wait. I'm sure they had a good laugh over the silly white woman.

## DARU

It was Sunday morning and we had just arrived in Daru, an island with a population of approximately twenty thousand in Western Province. Daru is a relatively modern society with refrigerated grocery markets, schools, a hospital, a prison, and a few motor vehicles. It was not uncommon for the churches in Daru to invite their YWAM guests to speak. Although it took me way out of my comfort zone, when asked to speak or when the Holy Spirit prompted me, I stood up, stepped out, and did the best I could. I was getting a lot of practice in the villages but somehow that felt different than in a church setting. I really wasn't too worried this particular morning as there was a large group of DTS students on board for this particular outreach and speaking at church was one of their assignments.

Of all the people on board, I was surprised to be one of a handful of people invited to attend a church service at the local prison. How crazy cool would that be? I could not turn down and opportunity like that. Of course, I'll go.

I was fascinated with the prison itself. Thirty men, young and old, sat outside under a large shade tree. Not far was the razor wire fence that surrounded the prison barracks. My eyes scanned the area and noticed only one uniformed guard. None of the inmates wore any particular prison garb to identify them as such. I heard many of them were serving time for murder. *How sad – all these men – tough on the outside but must be broken and hurt on the inside.* The worship team began to sing, and we joined the men on the tarp under the tree. How nice it was to have church outside the four walls.

All of a sudden, I knew without a doubt I was to speak to the prisoners. *Seriously, Lord? At a prison?!* I was not prepared. Where were the DTS students? After what seemed like an extremely short time of worship, I felt the prompting to stand up. Weak in the knees, hands shaking, and voice cracking, I began to speak. Pretty soon words were coming out of my mouth that were smarter than me. I could not gauge from the prisoners expressionless faces whether or not they understood my English or had been moved by God's word. We did not have an interpreter.

**I'm being stretched out of my comfort zone. I am thankful because it shows me that Jesus is truly my source – I could not do this on my own.**

After the service all of the men lined up and shook hands with each of us before they headed back into the confines of the razor wire fence.

## GRACE

Like a child, I wanted to cry and give up. I don't want to do this. I can't do this. I'm not good at flying by the seat of my pants. Help! Here I was supposed to be the team leader, and I was panicking. Our team was scheduled to travel by boat to another village for a week, but at the last minute the boat unexpectedly needed repairs and was out of commission. Therefore, we would have to spend the entire week in Daru. I was responsible for eleven people, the largest team I had had up to that point, and I had no clue what we were going to do all day long for five days. No contacts, no plans, no transportation, no map or directions to anything in the city, no flip charts or large heavy boxes of distribution items to lug around, and everyone looked to the leader for the itinerary. I wobbled a moment and prayed a pitiful "poor me help me" prayer.

I couldn't have asked for a more outgoing and bold group of young volunteers for this particular outreach. Not all volunteers are believers, but by God's grace, this entire group of DTS students were on fire for the Lord. And they were not afraid to show it. We walked to a large open field not far from the wharf where many a rugby game was played. The young men and women with me offered to lead songs and games, which is definitely not my forte, and it wasn't long until a crowd gathered to see what these foreigners were up to. Once they had everyone's attention (I can't say I had anything to do with it), they shared some health awareness talks and even came up with a malaria game on the spot to get everyone engaged. Young and old alike played a game of mosquito tag, which carried on for a good forty-five minutes.

While I cheered them on, three local men approached me, wondering who we were and what we were doing. Turns out they were involved in TB education and prevention. One fellow had just retired from working with World Vision and knew some key contacts on the island. He offered to be our walking guide to some of the many settlements located in and around the city. Not only was he our guide that day he set aside any plans he had for the whole week to accommodate us and introduce us to local organizations where we could share health awareness and the gospel. I was grateful, humbled, and saddened by my own selfishness as I watched him sacrifice his time for us. Would I even consider canceling my agenda for a week, or even a day, to serve a group of strangers who were on a mission, and for no compensation? I hate to answer my own question.

In one settlement, our guide gathered a group of young ladies and asked me to speak to them about respecting their bodies and saving sex until marriage. Teen pregnancies were on the rise, and they needed a heart-to-heart conversation. *Oh dear*, I felt I had just been rolled under the bus again and put on the spot, but I could not refuse.

I began with the first thing that came to mind, starting with my own story about Laurae and ending with what the Bible says. Our guide appeared to be satisfied; I wasn't so sure about the quiet audience though. I prayed for the girls, and we moved on.

God answered my distressed prayer that morning and saved the day. He is faithful and trustworthy, and I can do nothing apart from Him (Lamentations 3:22-23; Proverbs 3:5-6; John 15:5). How many times must He pick me up and plant my feet firmly on the ground before I get it? That broken boat had been His way to reveal Himself to me on a deeper level and to change me and my heart.

## THUD

Sweat covered my entire body. The mamas twirled their heavy hankies round and round to fan themselves and the sleeping infants in their laps. The thatched roof hut provided shade from the sun, but the heat inside was stifling as we flipped through the pages of our health awareness flip charts. Outside, squeals of laughter and children playing soccer could be heard but that didn't appear to distract the ladies from our teachings. Then came a loud thud. The flimsy hut floor shook slightly as the women shrieked and jumped to their feet. In all the commotion I observed a good-sized frightened lizard scurry to safety. The interpreter explained that snakes often hide and slither in the roofs of the huts and occasionally fall, just as the lizard had. Relieved, we all laughed nervously at the interruption.

From then on, I didn't just scan the ground and the trees for the Papuan black snake, the death adder, and the mighty python. I searched the ceilings as well.

God's hedge of protection was surely around us, protecting us from snakes, spiders, shongololos, crocodiles, jellyfish, mosquitos, sharks, waves, sickness, and tropical infections. Thank you, Lord!

## IN OVER MY HEAD

Dibora village was about a thirty-minute boat ride from where the YWAM PNG was anchored. One beautiful sunny morning, intense rays reflected off the calm seas and pods of dolphins frolicked nearby as if watching to see what a bunch of humans in a Falcon loaded with duffel bags and large plastic boxes were doing in their waters. I always looked forward to these longer jaunts to and from the villages. It was time to soak up the rays (not that I wasn't getting enough sunshine already), to pray, and to enjoy a few extra moments in paradise.

We had only one transport boat that morning. The other Falcon had taken a team on an overnight patrol. So for an hour and a half I scouted out the village and met with leaders while we waited for the rest of the team to arrive. Very few people were around for clinics. It was possible they did not receive word we were coming or had gotten the days mixed up. It was one of the rare days when we mostly played with the children and prayed with the adults. A nice change of pace, really.

A refreshing five-minute walk to the neighboring village of Kirikirikona left us more aware of our surroundings, as we were told stories of croc attacks and reports of people gone missing. Recently a young mother had been snatched and drug away. I was told that some villagers mark the location of an attack by anchoring poles in the mud at an angle over the water and hanging clothing from the tops.

As the workday came to an end, we waited on the shore for what seemed much longer than usual for our pickup shuttle boats to arrive. Apparently, a storm was brewing out at sea and the water was choppier than expected. It was imperative that we leave right away. I was extremely thankful that a coxswain with years of experience on the sea, was navigating the boat I had settled myself and my team in. We were given specific instructions on where and how to hang on, told to listen for directions, and to be prepared to get wet. He was calm in his deliverance so as not to alarm or frighten anyone, although a quick glance from the driver gave me the impression it was going to be a rough ride. The younger generation, who believe they are invincible, looked forward to a carnival ride. I myself never enjoyed a carnival and therefore positioned myself next to my seventy-year-old volunteer in the back of the boat where it was easier to hold on.

The sunset over the horizon was incredible as we made our way out into open water. I don't know what it was about the setting sun in that part of the world, but the radiant hues of red, orange, purple, and gold painted a supernatural masterpiece against the night sky that would make any artist envious. There is nothing like a PNG sunset. At first there was a lot of bouncing and jarring as we hit the incoming waves head on. I prayed and sang 'How Great is our God' as we entered deeper into the storm. (The wind and motor drowned out my voice, which was probably a good thing for those sitting near me.) I continued in prayer and song for the full ninety-minute trip. As the sunset faded and the skies turned darker, the swells grew higher. The coxswain accelerated to reach the top of a swell before the water broke and then slowed way down as we rode down the back side of the wave. His timing was perfect as we faced one giant wall of water after another.

At one point we got turned sideways and in the shadow of the dim running light we saw a ferocious pillar of water coming right toward us. I don't know about anyone else, but I braced myself for impact thinking *if I get thrown from the boat I could be bobbing around all night until I would be rescued in the morning—that is, unless a shark found me first.* Before I knew what had happened, I was covered with a heavy load of surprisingly warm salt water, and I was still in the boat, along with everyone else. Our driver maneuvered the Falcon through the swells like a pro, but a few times I secretly hoped for another tepid wave to crash over me and warm me up. The wind was chilly, and I shivered uncontrollably. Finally, in the distance, we saw the bright beacon of the ship. We arrived safely with all our gear, albeit drenched.

## SHOUT FROM THE MOUNTAIN TOPS

January 31, 2017, I received word that I was scheduled to go with a small team on an overnight helicopter patrol to Kira, a village in the highlands. *Oh my goodness!* The village was so remote that they had not received any kind of services for several years. My assignment was to teach health awareness topics, provide vision screening, distribute reading glasses, and give immunizations to babies and school children.

I can't lie; I was a bit nervous about the helicopter ride. That was something else I never desired to have on my bucket list. I think God has a sense of humor and penciled it on there just for fun when I wasn't looking. But how could I turn down an opportunity like that? Once more, the question: Who does this? And the answer: ME!

Crammed into a little bubble of a cockpit, the seven of us buckled up, put on our headgear to drown out the engine and propeller noise, and prepared for lift off. Surprisingly, I never felt the least bit nauseated and truly enjoyed the astonishing views through the glass bubble: Waterfalls, clear mountain springs, muddy rivers winding like snakes in the valleys, tiny villages, and gardens dotted the dense jungle below.

After a one-hour flight we landed on a grassy airstrip, hand mowed with a machete, I presume, near the top of the mountain. The natives had not known we were coming, but one of our local PNG doctors had been there before and some of the residents recognized him. How strange it must have been to see a helicopter show up one afternoon with six light-skinned strangers bringing medical supplies. They welcomed us graciously and invited us to stay and to bring the much-needed services. The village had an aid post and a couple of health volunteers but no supplies or medicine. The population of Kira was about three thousand people, but their homes were spread out and unseen in the bush. Only smoke from cooking fires rising above the canopy gave any clue of nearby civilization.

Kira has very nice and somewhat contemporary-looking guest houses constructed of milled lumber for visitor lodging. They were complete with screened windows, solid floors, a tin roof, and bathrooms with an actual porcelain commode (but no running water). Not what I was expecting at all. Supplies, I imagined, had to be air lifted in considering how remote the village was. I also wondered how often the residents of Kira had visitors to merit such nice accommodations. The locals lived in huts, but the guest house was very nice. I could've stayed there quite easily. It was cooler in the highlands but still warm enough that I didn't need a jacket. (When I worked at the school in Cañon, the kids made fun of me for always wearing a jacket at recess. I told them when the temperature turned eighty degrees, I would take off my coat.)

Two beautiful fourteen-year-old girls latched onto us straightaway. They were our helpers, tag-a-longs who could speak English quite well, which was a great asset throughout our visit. The father of one of the girls explained that Kira means "to shout out" in their local language. During WWII, he said, the inhabitants of Kira stood on top of the mountain and shouted to all the nearby villages, warning of possible danger. When I told him my granddaughter Esther's middle name was Kira, he surprised me with a special handmade child-sized *bilim* just for her.

We brought some back-up meal items like Emnaus and canned tuna and a water filter with us, not knowing what might be available. I never ceased to be amazed at the generous nature of the people of PNG. We were invited to share a meal with a family under their home. I'm pretty sure it was not their normal daily fare.

In the evening, we had a short time of worship under the stars, complete with guitars. I lived for moments like those. It was absolutely beautiful and surreal. The two tag-a-long girls insisted on having a sleepover with us. My memories of sleepovers were of late nights talking and giggling, eating junk food until I felt sick and then finally crashing when I could no longer keep my eyelids open. Apparently, time has not changed things. Squished together like sardines on the floor, we shared stories and laughed until some of us (namely, me) could no longer stay awake and called it a night. One of the girls flipped and flopped all night, jabbing me with an elbow here and a slap of the hand there, while a skinny leg draped across my waist. The odor of smoldering cooking fires mixed with hot sweaty perspiration filled my nostrils as I tried to sleep. I couldn't help but smile to myself at the thought of me at a slumber party in a high mountain jungle village in Papua New Guinea that just so happened to be named Kira. God was blessing me in ways I never could have imagined.

The next day our helpers led us to a pool of water in a jungle cave where we could bathe. Sliding down the muddy bank was a challenge, but the climb out was even more difficult as we tried to do so without needing another bath before reaching the dry grassy ground. The rest of the day was rainy and not many showed up for clinic, although there were enough people to make for steady work. I tested thirty-six people for reading glasses and enjoyed visiting with the villagers. The opportunity to stay in the village overnight made the visit so much more meaningful and memorable to me. I felt I had made connections, and when it was time to say goodbye, I wasn't just waving to faces and bodies, I was saying farewell to friends.

# EVE

"Adam, Adam, where are you? It's Eve. Who is taking care of baby Jesus? God is coming. Adam!" a woman's voice hollered over the lapping sound of the ocean waves. *Strange.* "Adam! I know you are up there," the voice came again. As far as I could remember, there was no one by the name of Adam on the ship of volunteers. And who would be yelling like that anyway?

We had just finished our evening meal and as usual many of us, me included, stood on the second level deck watching the last colorful hues of the sunset disappear as we enjoyed the warm ocean breeze. The voice was obviously not coming from anyone on board. It was not unusual to see a cluster of dugout canoes with curious natives staring at the big white boat in their waters, and it was not unusual to see fisherman out at twilight. But that was not the case on this night.

A small beam of light shone into the gloomy waters below revealed a naked lady bobbing in the waves with arms raised high in the air and hands clapping rapidly. She continued calling out for Adam, evidently believing he was on the ship somewhere. The commotion drew quite a crowd. Was she mad? Possessed? How did she get there? Many prayed while others stood staring in disbelief. The YWAM PNG was anchored in deeper waters far away from the shore. We were a five-minute ride in the Zodiac but an incredibly long way to swim. Eve did not appear to be drowning nor the least bit tired as she thrashed around yelling as loudly as she could. She exhibited superhuman strength and endurance. After the leaders deliberated, the captain decided to let down a boat to take her back to shore. Call it what you will, under demonic influence or mentally astray, this woman was not ok. When asked, the locals replied that she often exhibits strange behavior and to ignore her. The Land of the Unexpected took on another meaning that night.

## 100-YARD SQUELCH

We pulled into Pirupiru during high tide and unloaded all the gear just like we had in all the other villages we had visited that week.

It was fairly muddy and wet, and we had to navigate slippery logs to get to the village center. Thankfully, the young men, women, and children were more than helpful in getting us and our gear where we needed to be. The warm greetings and hospitality continued to touch my heart. Very humbling. But never was I so appreciative for their help than that day when it was time to haul our tubs, duffel bags, and supplies back to the Zodiacs at the end of a long hot day in the bush. I had heard stories about the long jaunts in the deep, deep mud, but had not yet experienced it.

In low tide our shuttle boats looked a long way off, at least three hundred feet, and I wondered how my knee would hold up. I scarcely noticed any discomfort as I followed my two teenage girl escorts. With each step, my foot slithered and sunk in the slime, finally stopping on a slick but firm solid layer. Miraculously, I stayed standing up and never lost my balance as did a few others. I squelched through the knee-deep quagmire (at times sinking nearly to my thighs), holding only my Teva sandals and my camera and stopping every so often to rest and take pictures. I hadn't laughed so much since my experience on the muddy jungle trail during IPHC. Who would have thought that a grandma in her mid-fifties would get so much enjoyment out of marching through a field of muck?

## IN CASE OF EMERGENCY

Being considered a long-term volunteer, I was elected to undergo emergency and security training while docked in the port town of Alotau. Approximately nine others were included in the written and hands-on education.

We partnered with members of the Alotau fire brigade one steamy afternoon and practiced putting out fires while wearing fireman's boots, pants, coat, headgear, and mask. First we used fire blankets, then foam and dry powder, and finally water from a heavy fire hose we pulled twenty-five yards on flat ground. I suddenly had a lot more respect for firefighters who do this for a living. It was all my partner and I could do to hang on to the hose when the water came rushing out. I definitely wasn't tough enough for that job. This was another time I couldn't believe I was doing such a thing, and in PNG of all places.

Back on board we had the privilege of dressing each other again in the heavy firefighting apparel. This time we were instructed to enter an artificially smoked-filled room with a buddy. We weren't able to see a thing, not even our partner. A dummy was hidden somewhere in the cabin in the hull of the ship, and we had to locate it and bring it out. We were given a radio in case we freaked out in the search. We didn't know the layout of the cabin as we crawled on hands and knees, feeling our way around. The smoke was harmless, but I admit it caused a bit of anxiety. I nearly aborted the mission before we finally found the "victim." In reality I think we only searched for a few minutes, but it seemed like much longer.

The training also included crowd control on the ship: how to reduce panic in an emergency situation and deal with hysterical individuals as we directed them to safety or onto a lifeboat. Personally, I preferred the smoke-filled room. I don't carry the confidence and authority needed to deal with a possible chaotic situation. I'm the one-on-one comforter not the commander-in-chief barking orders.

# SPUTUM

The ship manager pulled me aside one evening and informed me I would be moving to an empty cabin temporarily. My roomie was very sick, and after some testing, they decided it would be best to put her in quarantine for a couple weeks. They were concerned it might be tuberculosis (TB).

We would dock in Lae, one of the larger port cities with a hospital, for a few days. My cabin mate was scheduled for chest X-rays, and they recommend I go as well to have a doctor listen to my lungs. *Good grief.* I understood the need to be cautious since we all lived in close quarters, but I didn't think I was sick or contagious. *Besides*, I thought, *I am covered by the blood of Jesus. He took all my sickness and disease on the cross* (Psalm 103: 2-3). *If it eases the minds of the people on board I'll go.* I even agreed to hawk a loogie into a cup for the ship TB specialist.

The narrow entry to Lae Hospital had gray-and-white tile floors, pine green painted walls, and a couple rows of cafeteria-style chairs. The dark smiling faces behind the check-in counter were not strangers to YWAM, and they greeted us with their famous warm welcome. We waited quite some time to see the doctors. I met a lovely lady in the waiting area and learned that she had five daughters. I played silly hand games with her three-year-old and showed her photos on my tablet. The oldest daughter was not well at all. Her normally dark skin was freakishly pale. From what I understood, the majority of the people don't go to a hospital unless it's a life-or-death situation. While the family waited for the results of blood tests, I offered to pray for her, which was well received.

Finally, I was called in to see the doctor. A small room with an examination bed doubled as his office. His medical manuals, family photo, and other personal items were arranged on his desk. I looked at the same green walls as he interrogated me and listened intently to my lungs. He found nothing out of the ordinary. Just in case, he ordered some lab tests to rule out any infection due to possible exposure. I wasn't too keen on having blood taken and waiting another hour or more but considered it part of the experience. I had to wait for my roomie anyway, so there I sat on a hard chair outside the doctor's office door, pulling my feet in whenever a patient or nurse walked by.

Results revealed everything was within normal limits, and my hemoglobin was fine too. The doctor started to write a prescription for antibiotics, but I questioned his reasoning and refused the order. Instead, he prescribed thirty days' worth of vitamin C and eight to ten glasses of water. Perfect. My personal stash of vitamin C was getting low, and it was hard to find outside the cities. Thirty- seven US dollars later I was on my way home. Once back on board I was informed my sputum looked good. Ha. *Yuck!*

## DIVINE PROTECTION

There is no way of knowing for sure how many times God protected all of us from harm's way during those eight months. Consider all the boat trips to and from villages plus getting in and out of bobbing vessels; the threat of crocs, snakes, spiders, shongololos, coral reefs, stingers and sharks; the rickety bridges, ladders, and mud-covered logs; not to mention unfamiliar foods, witchcraft, and exposure to tropical illnesses. He must have been working overtime because there were very few incidents that were of a serious nature. What situations did occur could have been much worse if we hadn't believed that the Almighty was watching out for us (Joshua 1:9, Psalm 121:7-8).

One afternoon the team leaders were made aware of possible dangerous conditions ahead. The boat master wanted everyone loaded onto the return boats to leave Bina Village by 4:00 p.m. By the time the last baby immunization was given, though, and all supplies repacked, farewells said, and all the volunteers in the Falcon, it was well after 5:00. The tide was extremely low, making it difficult to maneuver among the mud banks. The strain to see the random branches and logs floating in the shallow waters increased as the sun began to set. The YWAM PNG captain himself left his command in a small boat to come find us and to guide us back to the ship. There was serious concern about the bore tide that comes in each evening around 6:30. I knew nothing about bore tides at the time, but apparently if you did not know what you were doing, a boat could easily be capsized and the occupants washed away and drowned. So I sang worship songs and prayed for our safety, as did the other clinic leader who sat facing me from the other side of the boat. Thanks be to God all three boats arrived safely but not without a few choice words from the Papua New Guineans on board. They knew firsthand the dangers of being on the river at that time of day, and we definitely heard about it. Heed the directions of the boat master.

# ONLY IN FAIRY TALES

**It can't get much better than this. Working, resting, openly worshipping in a place that is about as close to paradise on earth as you can get. Oh my, I am so blessed.**

The long squelch through the mud was an unforgettable, joyous memory, but I was in seventh heaven the day I got to go off the beaten path in the jungle. I wanted to laugh, cry, shout for joy, and raise my hands in thanksgiving (although I needed my hands just in case) for the trek of a lifetime in our new outreach location in Milne Bay.

After a very pleasant day assisting the optometry team with vision screenings and touring yet another unique village nestled in a valley of rocks and caves, I was invited to walk back to the wharf rather than take the PMV (private motor vehicle) used for transporting larger numbers of people. Any chance to walk, I was all for it. It would take over an hour they said, since we'd be trekking through the dense jungle. And I might get wet. So be it. Let's go.

Two Papua New Guinean crew members, me, and a few half naked children, left the heavily rutted road and meandered down a narrow grass-covered trail into the thick undergrowth of the tropical rain forest. I didn't walk nearly as fast as my leaders, whom I trusted to know where they were going, because I sure didn't. For one, I wanted to take in everything around me, and two, I didn't want to make a wrong step. We went up and down steep rocky ravines moist with jungle dew and dark from the dense canopy overhead. The youngsters stayed close and pointed out the best places to plant my feet and what rocks or vines to grab hold of. Astonishing caves and coral outcroppings lined either side of the trail. Mini waterfalls fell into the cool streams that we waded through more than once. Oh, my goodness, I was living a dream!

We made our way up a small hill and, to my surprise, we came across a shanty hut built at the entrance of a large cave. A man sat alone on a fence that surrounded the property. He nodded and smiled as we drew near. The children explained the gentleman was mute and the cave was his home. He lived by himself and motioned for us to take a look. I felt a bit uneasy about intruding into his private space, so I satisfied myself by peeking in from a distance. Not much to see really. We prayed for the jungle hermit and continued our mission back to the ship. It was hot and muggy, and the air smelled of a combination of fishy saltwater and ripe organic soil. So amazing. Story books had come alive, and I didn't want this story to end.

# 21

## MEANWHILE, BACK IN THE USA

ews from home since the beginning of the year was sporadic and not all that uplifting. I was sad and discouraged. Thousands of miles away from my family, I had to totally put my trust in the Lord and prayer.

## MOM

Mom had been isolating herself, not eating properly, and the pain in her hip and leg was increasing. A neighbor lady checked in on her often and took her meals and then reported back to my sister. It was time for an evaluation. Unfortunately, the diagnosis was dementia, and the prognosis was that it would progress quickly. We had all suspected it. It kind of left a pit in my stomach. *Lord, lift her up and protect her from harm. I pray for joy and hope but also a burning desire to come over her to know You and call out Your name as her Lord and Savior. I trust You.*

Mom also had been in the ER twice with severe pain in her leg. She was adamant about not wanting or needing outside help, but almost in the same sentence she told my sister: "These people (meaning the people in PNG) are not as important as me, and Holly needs to come home and take care of me."

Oh my goodness, what a guilt trip. But at the same time, even though I had peace about staying, I did have some doubts. I was either avoiding the situation by distancing myself by being on the ship, or I had God's peace knowing this was where I was supposed to be right now. *Am I fooling myself?* I thought. *Is the enemy at work? Am I cold hearted? Why am I questioning?* The few people I talked to had different opinions. But really, I knew I should not be listening to them. I needed to seek God (Matthew 6:33). My obedience is to God, not my mom or the opinions of man. I was totally willing to go back now or in the future. *Not my will but Yours be done* I prayed. I knew God wouldn't love me any less if I went home, but if I did and it wasn't His will, then I would be disobedient. *God is so much bigger than this,* I thought. *He knows exactly what is going on and the outcome. Who am I to decide what is best? Lord I choose to trust You, lay my Mom at Your feet and surrender. I trust that if and when I should go home You will make it absolutely clear to me and give me peace. I am Yours.*

Eventually, signs indicated Mom most likely would need round-the-clock care. She was no longer safe at home alone. She was fearful and angry when the three of us kids suggested an assisted living facility, but it had to be done and fairly soon.

## LAURAE

Adrenal fatigue and severe depression. (I really don't like those words!) Laurae was unable to eat or sleep. She was pregnant with baby number three, who was growing well, but Laurae herself had not gained any weight in a couple of weeks. She barely had energy to shower let alone give birth. The midwives expressed concerns about doing a home birth unless she got better. Laurae said she was not worried, anxious, or fearful, but she was very sad. She was to meet with a prenatal psychiatrist for an assessment. To make a difficult situation worse, a friend of hers who was expecting within weeks of Laurae's due date died suddenly of an infection that went septic. It was painfully hard to teach and minister in the villages when you knew your baby girl was suffering back home. *Why Lord? Why her right now?* Did I really think He couldn't handle this, that He didn't love her more than me? Be still and know that the Creator of the universe is in control. I prayed for healing and safety for both Laurae and baby.

Technology frustrates me, but I was grateful to have learned how to do FaceTime. It brought so much joy to see Syris and little Esther and to hear their sweet little voices. It was music to my ears.

I was in some of the most unexplored and remote places in the world! Not that I was complaining at all, but I wondered why. Sometimes I wondered if God just brought me there to bless me with beauty, adventure, things I never dreamed I'd ever do just because He loves me. Maybe He brought me there to get me away from home, so I would have to rely on Him for everything and to care for my family.

**Rejoice always. Pray without ceasing. Be thankful in all circumstances for that is the will of God for me. Rejoice. Rejoice and quit trying to figure things out. It's all in God's hands.**

Finally, on May 15 (several weeks before I returned to the states), I received word that I had a new granddaughter. Both Laurae and baby Rena Eden were doing well. Good news always refreshes my soul and lifts me up. I hurt when my family hurts; I rejoice when they rejoice. Thank you, Lord, for the gift of life!

# 22

## |GROWING WEARY|

I was tired. My muscles and joints ached all night, and I just didn't want to do it again. I wanted to go home, but I had no home to go to at that moment. I wasn't ready to give up PNG, I just needed a break. I needed to step back and process from a new perspective. Ship life was wearing on me: different diet, lack of good exercise, no privacy or quiet time. Lord, *I have to trust in Your strength, and in Your plans and purpose for me.*

Being on the go constantly with little rest physically and spiritually can lead to burnout, and I felt I was on my way. Or maybe it's also because I am twice the age of most of the other team leaders, and they limit their stay on the ship to two or three outreaches, not nine.

The ship clinic leader recognized my need for a day of respite and arranged a ride for me to go to the Port Moresby Nature Park while we docked between outreaches. The park is like a botanical garden and wildlife sanctuary all in one. My kind of place!

Periodically, I was overwhelmed with emotion (surprise!) and could not hold back the tears. A combination of being overly tired and wowed by the amazing grace and favor God bestowed upon me.

I heard that PNG was home to one-third of the world's population of bird species (and bugs), but so far I had only seen a few in their natural habitat. What a treat it was to walk through Port Moresby's giant aviary and see up close the uncaged beauties flitting from tree to tree or watching me with heads cocked. They were some of the most colorful and unique birds I'd ever seen, all in one place. I even captured a photo of the exotic bird-of-paradise. Absolutely glorious!

Out of nowhere came a large Papua Green Parrot who decided my shoulder was a good place to land. I wasn't sure how to react. My ears were exposed, and I half expected a nip at any moment. Instead, I felt his talons grip my scalp as he climbed onto my head. Evidently, my green feathered hitch-hiker was interested in my sunglasses. While tapping the dark lenses, he accompanied me for quite some time as I wandered and gazed at God's winged creation.

Small gray wallabies hopped playfully around in their designated habitat, while the odd-looking tree kangaroo sat slothfully in a tree, oblivious to her surroundings. With a rat-like face, pointed ears and a long, mostly hairless tail she looked more like a large rodent. Although she had a pouch, she didn't resemble a kangaroo in the least.

The trees, flowers, shrubs and ornamental foliage were the huge highlights of my day. I used to collect houseplants of all kinds, the more unusual the better. Before I traveled to Townsville for IPHC I had to sell or find loving homes for all of them. What amazed me is the mysterious ways God orchestrates the simple pleasures in our lives, so that many of my favorite specimens from home were on display right before me, growing in PNG.

When Jedd and Laurae were little, I came across the most unusual tree in a greenhouse in Colorado, and I couldn't leave without it. I'd never seen anything like it before, nor since then—until that day in Port Moresby. The only name I ever knew it by was Monkey Puzzle. It resembles a Norfolk pine in shape but instead of needles, its branches are lined with hundreds of small leaves similar to a handsaw blade without the uniformity in size. Just like the edge of a saw, the leaves are quite sharp. I kept mine in the house, and it had grown to be about five feet tall. The tree I came across on my walk through the nature park towered way above my head, and the trunk was almost too big to wrap my arms around. Whoever in a million years would have thought I'd find myself where they grow naturally?

It's amazing what a day can do to restore, re-energize, and motivate a woman to keep on going, one step at a time.

# 23

## | BITTERSWEET |

ay 23, 2017, was a day filled with mixed emotions. It was my last boat transfer to a Papua New Guinea village. I felt grief at that realization but at the same time, relief. I was worn out and longed to see my family and hold my precious new granddaughter, but I dreaded the idea of having to remain in the states for any length of time.

My taste buds craved a huge spinach salad with a variety of veggies and a slice of real whole wheat bread loaded with nuts and seeds. Sadly, I would miss the juicy ripe mangoes, fresh coconut, kau kau, pit pit, and cooked ibica greens. Oh, and the fresh baby bananas, papaya, and pineapple. I loved PNG—the people, the climate, the simple yet challenging lifestyle. My stomach churned when I remembered the glitz, glamor, and materialistic posh living to which I would return. The more, more, more, me, me, me society. The thing I would miss the most was residing, working, and doing life each day among a body of believers who take prayer seriously, who seek and trust God in all circumstances. For that I am truly blessed and grateful.

It was lovely to spend a few days back in Townsville before the long series of flights back to Colorado. It was a good readjustment period, a chance to begin adapting to reverse culture shock. The mingled smells of concrete and plumeria filled the air. Cars, sirens, and the beep, beep, beep of street crossing signals reminded me I was no longer in the bush. I have to admit I was happy to sleep in a bigger bed, to have my own space to hang out and cook my own meals. Time to reflect on the past eight months and God's purpose in it all would come later and would take much longer than a few days. For the time being I just wanted to rest.

The desire for rest became clear as I compiled the statistics for my nine outreaches as Community Engagement Leader. The results were extraordinary.

1. Visited over 90 villages in 5 provinces.

2. Led 18 orientations for volunteers.

3. Trained 5 CE leaders.

4. Met about 900 volunteers from all over the world.

5. Attended approximately 120 team/staff meetings.

6. Spent over 100 hours recording stats and reports.

7. Inventoried the resource area 10 times and restocked from supplies in freight containers.

8. Participated in 10 to 12 hours of fire safety training.

9. Prayed for hundreds of individuals.

10. Interviewed 50 plus village elders, teachers, or pastors for village assessments.

11. Taught a minimum of 180 health education sessions and gospel messages.

12. Endured roughly 35 sails.

13. Gave over 100 vaccinations/immunizations.

14. Screened a multitude for reading glasses.

15. Two overnight patrols, 1 helicopter and 1 boat.

16. Survived a harrowing boat ride in high seas in the dark.

17. Engaged children and adults in 360 songs of "Head, Shoulders, Knees and Toes."

18. One cough, 1 RDT for malaria, 1 trip to Lae Hospital, and no major injuries.

Whew! That doesn't include cleaning and inventory of the dental clinic and ophthalmology lab, an occasional dinner clean-up in the galley, acting as tour guide for visitors on the ship, sorting piles and piles of donated clothes, or the weekly chore of doing the team's laundry.

Spiritually, I grew tremendously in certain areas and developed deeper levels of understanding in others. I continue to grow in maturity and wisdom as over time God reveals more of His character, will, and purpose in this wild and wonderful adventure. There are eight areas I can identify as obvious fields of growth, although I'm still reflecting and getting revelation even today from this experience. I needed to learn

1.  what it means to surrender my will and worries to God.

2.  how to receive and rest in the Father's unconditional love.

3.  to rely and trust in the power of prayer.

4.  to trust that God's ways and thoughts are bigger and better than my own.

5.  to recognize and acknowledge God's glory and unsurpassed beauty in His creation.

6.  there is literal power of life and death in the tongue.

7.  my identity and authority is in Christ Jesus.

8.  to be bold and not afraid of taking risks.

What and honor and privilege it is to follow Jesus.

One night I could not sleep. I lay awake thinking how my life and testimony resembled the building of our house in the mountains near Westcliffe. It started at the bottom with a solid foundation. The walls were next. Some are Styrofoam blocks, some cordwood, and some strawbales. There were flaws in all. Windows concealed and exposed. Inside there were many rooms with different activities going on at the same time, with different people coming and going and family always there. There was plumbing that needed to fit and connect properly so that water flowed smoothly. Sometimes it plugged up, ran slowly, or the temperature was not regulated. And in all the walls were unseen wires connecting all the rooms together in ways we were unaware, but it all tied together in the end. Outside there was a garden where seeds were planted and nurtured. Sometimes we saw the fruit, but many times plants don't mature for one reason or another: not enough life-giving water, weather/storms, animals and creepy crawly critters, neglect, disease, but there is hope and excitement for the next season. *God is my foundation – without Him I have no dwelling place.* Through life's experiences the walls of our lives are built. Though they seem sturdy, sometimes they leak, crumble, go through fire and storms. If they're not mended the same issues will resurface again and again. They become weaker and unable to repair unless you start the building process over: new creation, born again. The old baggage must be dealt with and left behind, carrying it into a new house is not healthy. Not that new issues won't arise, but if God surrounds us within the new walls and covers us with a solid roof, we are safe in His dwelling place and can weather the storms in His protection. And all the while, inside the walls, God is connecting the wires and stories in our lives in ways we never could have imagined. For our good and His glory. *He is my Rock, my fortress, my hope. In Him I am secure and in Him is my dwelling place* (Psalm 91).

# 24

## "YOU SHOULD WRITE A BOOK"

*Lord, I thank You for today. I thank You for my past and how
You brought me out of the darkness and into the light. How
You have blessed me and my family in so many ways. Thank
You for being true to Your word and providing for all of our
needs. Lord, thank You for the person I am today. The hard
times, good times, and the times in the wilderness, to love me,
teach me, and to grow me in my faith and trust. Lord, I bless
what You've done, what You are doing, and what You will still
do. All the praise and glory belong to You.*

I had ample opportunities to share my story in the villages, on
walks, working and living on the ship, and whenever I felt the
Spirit lead. I was amazed at how many times someone said:
"You should write a book." Kind of like when God pursued me in
the beginning, sending a little girl with pigtails to tell me about
her church with "coffee and donuts!" And how every time I turned

around, I would see or hear "Vineyard." Could it be that my vision of the red book in my dream several years earlier really was something I was supposed to write? Surely not! I don't know the first thing about writing a book nor was it ever on my radar to do so. *Oh, my!*

Repeatedly, during my long flights home, a nagging thought entered my mind. I sensed the Holy Spirit directing me to meet up with a specific woman when I got back to Cañon City. A poised and godly lady, and not someone I met with regularly. Actually, I didn't meet with her at all unless it was church or business related. I didn't have a problem asking her to join me for lunch when I got home, and she didn't hesitate to accept the invitation. What did God have up His sleeve with this meeting?

I arrived a bit early at the café and chose a booth next to a sunny window. Several people entered and took their places as I waited with anticipation. Standing tall and confident, dressed casually professional, the pretty dark-haired woman scanned the dining area. I stood up and smiled as she walked my direction. "Holly! Welcome back. How are you?" She said joyfully.

Sitting down, she looked me directly in the eye and asked. "So when are you going to write that book?"

Seriously! That was the first thing she said. *OK God, I get it.*

# 25

## ‖ STANDING UP ‖

Thank goodness I chose to keep a journal for the last twelve years of my life, and continue to do so. As I began to read, write, and relive my struggles, heartaches, questions, and distress, I realized God had given me specific Scripture references at specific times that brought me direction, hope, joy, and peace. I guess you would say they are my life verses.

### PSALM 46:10

*"Be still and know that I am God. I will be exalted among the nations, I will be exalted in the earth!"* In the course of a dog attack, a case of West Nile Virus, two serious car accidents, a teenage pregnancy, and the diagnosis of a furiously evil cancer, which took Jedd's life, I had unexplainable peace and many moments of joy.

## ROMANS 8:28

*"And we know that for those who love God all things work together for good, for those who are called according to his purpose."* This verse was impressed upon my heart and highlighted as we prayed for Jedd's healing and into the years ahead. The call to a Discipleship Training School and then my return to a job I wasn't crazy about at exactly the time when Laurae and Syris needed a place of refuge. A wedding, a divorce, my own cancer diagnosis, and an uncomfortable and unforgettable assignment into medical missions. I chose to believe that even though I couldn't see the outcome, I knew God was sovereign and good, that one day I could look back and be thankful for the work He has done.

## 1 THESSALONIANS 5:16-18

*"Rejoice always, pray without ceasing, give thanks in all circumstances; for this is the will of God in Christ Jesus for you."* I took this convicting piece of Scripture seriously as a command. He did not tell me to do these things if I wanted to. I admit that being thankful with a positive attitude was not always easy while I trained for IPHC and my return venture on the YWAM PNG. Every choice we make (positive or negative) has a consequence. I became more aware of the thoughts I was thinking and the motives of the words that followed those thoughts. Was I speaking life or was I speaking death over myself and others? Was I rejoicing, praying, and being thankful in all circumstances?

Being in parts of the world where sorcery and witchcraft are common practice, putting on the armor of God was a necessity. I know now that this is also necessary daily any time we attempt to stand up and step out in faith to do the will of God. The enemy will do everything in his power to thwart all those plans and good intentions. Jesus said, "The thief comes only to steal and kill and destroy, I came that they may have life and have it abundantly" (John 10:10). We are to resist the devil and not be afraid. We have been given the authority and power through Christ Jesus to destroy all the works and plans of the enemy (2 Timothy 1:7, James 4:7, Luke 10:19). I am tired of watching Satan and his cohorts destroy lives when we have all the fullness of God living within us (1 John 4:4). We, as believers, are overcomers, victorious, beloved children of God whom He loves with an everlasting love (1 John 5:4, Revelations 21:7, 2 Thessalonians 2:16, Jeremiah 31:3).

This brings me to Ephesians 6:10-20.

Finally, be strong in the Lord and the strength of his might. Put on the whole armor of God, that you may be able to stand against the schemes of the devil. For we do not wrestle against flesh and blood, but against rulers, against the authorities, against the cosmic powers over this present darkness, against the spiritual forces of evil in the heavenly places. Therefore, take up the whole armor of God, that you may be able to withstand in the evil day, and having done all, to stand firm. Stand therefore, having fastened on the belt of truth, and having put on the breastplate of righteousness, and, as shoes for your feet, having put on the readiness given by the gospel of peace. In all circumstances take up the shield of faith, with which you can extinguish all the flaming darts of the evil one; and take the helmet of salvation, and the sword of the Spirit, which is the word of God, praying at all times in the Spirit, with all prayer and supplication. To that end keep alert with all perseverance, making supplication for all the saints, and also for me, that words may be given to me in opening my mouth boldly to proclaim the mystery of the gospel, for which I am an ambassador in chains, that I may declare it boldly, as I ought to speak.

I am standing today only by the grace of God. I am choosing to live a life acceptable and pleasing to God to the best of my ability, with my current limited understanding of the Bible, seeking the Holy Spirit for wisdom and truth, and to clothe myself with the full armor God has given me, so that when the end draws near, I will remain *Standing Up*.

# 26

## | ARE YOU SEARCHING? |

If you have not yet asked Jesus to be your Lord and Savior, please keep reading. This will be the most important life decision you will ever make. All of us, every single one of us, falls short of the glory of God, and there is nothing we, in ourselves, can do to earn our way into heaven. If you have heard that all roads lead to heaven, you have been misled. Jesus is the only way to the Father. Acts 4:12 says there is "no other name under heaven given among men by which we may be saved." We are saved by grace through faith, not by our good deeds. Even while we were sinners, Jesus died on the cross. His blood was shed for you and me so that we may have eternal life with Him. God is all about love and having a relationship with His children. None of us are a mistake. He knew us before we were even conceived. Nothing we have ever done, no sin, is so big that He will not forgive us if we ask for forgiveness in faith. Even faith the size of a mustard seed can move mountains. We must repent and turn away from old sinful behavior and trust Jesus to fulfill His good plans for us.

I'd be lying if I said it will be easy and all your troubles will cease. You probably have figured that out by reading my story so far. Life includes hardship. But I will tell you that your perspective and response to the situations in your life will be dramatically different when you have a relationship with Jesus. Deep within our beings, we all desire to be loved unconditionally, to have peace and comfort in our hearts through trying times, and to know an unexplainable joy despite life's battles. It can only be found in Jesus, and it surpasses all reasonable understanding. God is way beyond human reasoning, and unless you stand, take the step of faith, and call upon the Name of Jesus, you won't experience the supernatural. It's not a feeling or an event that can be explained or described; it's a divine transformation and a continual renewing of the mind. Our God is such an awesome God. Won't you make that decision today to ask Jesus to come into your heart and life before it is too late? We are not guaranteed a tomorrow, or even another hour. Remember, there is power of life and death (eternal) in our words, so say this prayer out loud as a confession of faith:

Dear Jesus, I humbly come before You now and acknowledge I have made ungodly choices in my life and have sinned against You. I am truly sorry, and I ask for Your forgiveness. Please come into my heart and guide me as my Lord and Savior. I believe You were born and lived as a man and then paid the ultimate price, a horrible death on a cross, for my ransom. I believe You were buried and after three days God raised You from the dead so that I myself may have eternal life. Thank you, Father, that You loved me so much You sent Your only son to die for me. I believe I am saved and the old me has passed away. I am now a new creation in Christ. All glory, honor, and praise be to God. Amen.

My prayer and encouragement for you as you begin this incredible journey is to find a Bible believing church, preferably one that offers prayer ministry. Start fellowshipping with other believers and get involved. Purchase a Bible with a commentary, a study Bible, if you do not already have one and dive in.

I pray God blesses you according to His plans and purposes for you as a willing son or daughter of the Most High God. May He guard your heart, mind, will, and emotions as you step forward with hope and anticipation of your God-given assignment(s). I bless what He has already begun in your life and know that whatever He has started He will bring to completion.

Hallelujah! It is well. Now you too have the strength to remain standing up in the end.

# AFTERWORD

## MY BIRTH PLACE, OF ALL PLACES

Before my stint in PNG came to an end, I knew God wanted me back in Colorado. "Trust Me," He said. Why is it that whenever I hear those words I get an uncomfortable feeling in the very center of my being? In my mind I believed I would find a small apartment in Grand Junction to help relieve my sister from some of the duties related to our mom's care. Although Mom resided in an assisted living memory care unit, it seemed there were endless doctor, dental, and specialized care appointments she needed to be chauffeured to. Her strength and mobility had declined quite quickly while I was gone, and the task of getting her in and out of a vehicle was an ordeal in itself. I was a bit excited and looked forward to having a space of my own in Grand Junction's lovely, warm (some would say hot) climate with the possibility of having a small garden.

For some reason beyond me, God kept nudging me toward Gunnison. Gunnison?! *Rugabugs!* He knows I strongly dislike those long cold winters! When I moved away over thirty- five years ago, I vowed never to live there again. I was born and raised in that small community and some of my greatest and some of my worst memories originated there. Not that there is anything wrong with Gunny, as the locals refer to it. It truly is a remarkable and beautiful place—to visit. However, if I learned anything over the years, I learned that it is always in my best interest to obey God's leading, always—whether Holly likes it or not.

My father still made Gunnison his home, and he very graciously opened up his house for me to stay as long as I needed or wanted. I accepted his invitation, believing it to be temporary. Thankfully, Grand Junction was just a short two-and-one-half-hour drive away from my mom and sister, and I was able to visit often.

A couple years ago I sent my mother a card telling her I loved her but more importantly that Jesus loved her. I wanted her to know and experience His love too. My sister was there to read the message to her, and in a twenty-minute period of lucidity, of total soundness of mind, she sincerely wanted to know this Jesus and received Him as her Lord and Savior. Hallelujah!

I didn't know how long I would be planted in Gunnison (still don't), so I reluctantly began to look for a job. Honestly, I didn't want to be employed. I didn't want to be tied down when God called me back to the mission field. Foolish thinking!

## HOUSEKEEPERS WANTED

Each time I scanned the Help Wanted ads, the words *housekeepers wanted* jumped out at me. I remembered watching how hard the head housekeeper on the YWAM PNG worked, and I had been so grateful I was not in her shoes. I tried hard to ignore the persistent call for housekeepers, and I prayed as I perused the rest of the ads asking God to clearly show me what kind of work He would have me do. It took a chipmunk to confirm His desire.

In Gunnison, I rely on long walks in nature to open myself to God's instructions for me, just as I had on Skyline Drive in Cañon City, when my life had fallen apart and before all my travels began. On a beautiful sunny day, on a hiking trail near Blue Mesa Lake, a particular chipmunk caught my attention. I have seen hundreds, if not thousands, of these busy little mammals in my lifetime, but that particular day I felt compelled to observe closely as he worked. I suddenly sensed a mysterious desire to spend some time researching these critters. I learned a number of interesting facts about chipmunks, but it wasn't until I saw the meaning of its scientific name that God's persistent help wanted messages to me were validated: *Tamias* (from the Greek ταμίας) means "steward," "treasurer," and "*housekeeper*."

*Good grief.*

At the same time, I prayed often about which church God would have me attend. He led me to one which would not have been my first choice. But what does Holly know? It didn't take long to realize that it was neither the pastor nor the sermons but the people in the congregation that God so beautifully orchestrated for me to meet. Within the first couple of weeks, a woman invited me for coffee. About thirty minutes into our visit, I learned that my hostess and her husband owned a business, and they wondered if I would be interested in some part-time work. You guessed it, doing housekeeping!

Instead of being grateful for what the Lord was doing in my life, I found myself grumbling and complaining. One year into my "captivity," as I power-walked a local trail, God spoke clearly to me:

"You're not going anywhere until your book is finished." What?! Head and shoulders drooping and pouting like a three-year-old, I stomped my way home. Writing is hard, much harder than I expected, even when it is my life story, and I don't have to make anything up. I could have chosen to cut corners, go cheap, and just get it done. But the Bible says that no matter what you do, you are to "work heartily as for the Lord and not for men" (Colossians 3:23). Looked like I was going to call Gunnison home for a while.

One year later and still grumbling, I told God how miserable I was and how I wished I was back in PNG or some other place He might call me to go—as if there had been some divine mistake. I did not expect His response, but boy oh boy, it shut me up. "How do you expect Me to send you someplace else when you can't be grateful where you are?" *Ouch*! I've since come into a deeper level of surrender and have succumbed to the fact that Gunnison may be my final destination this side of heaven. I'm ok with that now. "It is no longer I who live but Christ who lives in me" (Galatians 2:20).

Honestly, I am extremely blessed to be here, and it just took me some time to recognize it. When I finally took my eyes off myself, there was a shift in perspective. My housekeeping jobs are flexible, which allows me time to travel to Grand Junction to visit my mom and sister regularly, as well as time to write. Only in God's economy could I work fourteen hours a week and bring home a bigger paycheck than I did working full-time for twelve years in the school system. It was enough money to move out of my father's home and into a rental he has in the middle of town. I had a space of my own. The super tiny backyard, unkept and littered with construction trash when I moved in, is now a tidy but abundant garden. Last season, it provided fresh veggies not only for me but fed family and friends as well. It was so nice to play in the dirt again—a dream come true.

And my dream of a grandma's house also came to pass. The empty basement has been remodeled into a play haven for my grandchildren, Laurae's three kids. It even has an indoor treehouse for Syris and a kitchen underneath the floor of the treehouse for Esther and Rena.

I am overjoyed to say that Laurae, and family are currently living nearby. I can't begin to express what a blessing it is to have my grandkids so close for the time being. They light up my life. Laurae is currently working on writing a book to empower and encourage women based on her experience and God's redemptive power.

My husband and I divorced on civil terms, and though we went our separate ways, I am satisfied to say we remain great friends today.

Just recently God has given me a vision for a house of prayer in good ole Gunny. How and when this victory will take place is under His sovereign authority. In anticipation and expectation, I long to see in this valley a revival and an awakening—the manifest glory of God—and with it, salvation, healing, and deliverance. It is a privilege and an honor to serve the Lord of lords and King of kings.

To any of Jedd's friends who may be reading this by chance or by divine placement, I want you to know you are being brought before the Lord regularly in prayer. I am committed to pray for you until you come into a genuine saving grace relationship with Jesus. I hope it doesn't take dire circumstances for you to drop to your knees, like it did for me, but at the same time I pray for whatever it takes.

You, and all of you, are that loved, that valuable, and that worthy.

# ABOUT THE AUTHOR

HOLLY CONWELL is passionate about seeing people healed, restored, and living in victory and the fullness of God. A daily journey worth standing up for. *Standing Up* is her first book, and she is currently working on a couple children's books. Holly is a grandmother of three and lives in Colorado.

She is available to speak on missions, love and loss and joy in tribulation based on her experiences, Scripture, and personal testimony. For more information, questions, and to request a speaking engagement please visit her website at standinginvictory.me.

CPSIA information can be obtained
at www.ICGtesting.com
Printed in the USA
FSHW010052250521
81789FS

9 781947 360945